If You Fall Down Seven Times Get Up Eight

七転八起

by Deshi, PhD

Aspects of Practice for Gay and Lesbian Buddhists

ISBN 978-0-646-59496-5

Electronically published by BookCyclone.

Cover Design by Deshi.

For my sweetie
and
with gratitude to my teachers and sangha

Contents

1
Introduction
What This Book is About

One of my favorite pastimes is trawling Amazon to see what new Buddhist books are out there, especially those which have a practical bent or tackle a gritty problem. I love reading the reviews, blurbs and content pages. It gives me great pleasure to see Buddhism working and adapting itself to modern life. During one of my trawling sessions, it occurred to me that I'd never looked for books written by and for gay people. Gay people and Buddhism in the West are well suited to each other, and I expected this to be reflected in scores of stories, journals, practical guides and teachings. The result was anything but this. In fact, we can hardly find ourselves in print!

There are an extremely limited number of books about our Buddhist practice and the Dharma,[1] and what currently exists cannot offer a variety of views on what it means to be both gay and Buddhist. Almost all are very general with no books specifically for beginners on the Path. Women are also under-represented since most focus on the experience of men or sacred texts and sexuality. This is really unfortunate because some of us need help, and there is almost nothing out there in print to do it.

We need help precisely because of who we are. At some point in our lives, every gay person experiences prejudice, fear, injustice, rejection and confusion. We may not experience all of these things all of the time, but it is a good bet that some portion of our lives will be devoted to working out how to live as a gay person in a heterosexual world. Sometimes this is no easy task and the lack of books by gay Buddhists makes this even harder. This is the prime reason why I decided to write this book — to provide suggestions for which parts of the Path can help us look suffering in the eye and breathe it.

---

[1] Dharma — the teachings of the Buddha.

I am firmly convinced that Buddhism is especially well suited to gay people. There are a variety of aspects of Buddhist practice which can help us transcend our own ego and the bigotry of others. From my own experience I know that it can provide us with a veritable suite of angles with which to view our own suffering, and a large repertoire of practical guidelines for action in our daily lives. This book outlines with concrete examples several different reasons why Buddhism and gay people are a good match.

I am not a Dharma teacher. As a gay person and Buddhist practitioner however, I am completely comfortable in stating how the dharma and practice can help gay people. I know what can help because I know what has worked in my own life. It is from this perspective that I am writing. This is why this book describes the advantages for gay people of the what and why of practice. To give detailed instructions of the how, that is, the proper spiritual methods for employing and assessing those aspects, is not the focus.

Buddhism can also help not only gay people but anyone who suffers from victimization and a feeling of separation due to who they are. So this book is also food for thought for anyone whose daily practice is in an environment of intolerance and prejudice. If you want to give straight dharma friends a book which sheds light on some of the difficulties gay people face, then this book may enlighten them. *Sanghas*[2] can also use it as a general reference book.

Please also note that while the title mentions gay and lesbian Buddhists, the term gay in this book refers to both men and women. There are a variety of words I might have used as a cover term for our sexuality and there is no consensus amongst us as to which one is the best. I am not fond of queer, for example. For brevity's sake and because gay is ubiquitously used for both genders, I have chosen this word for both.

The title *If You Fall Down Seven Times Get Up Eight* (*nana korobi ya oki* in Japanese) has great meaning for me. It is a proverb used as encouragement to persevere, and is closely associated with the

---

[2] Buddhist communities.

mammoth nine year sitting effort of the First Patriarch of Chinese Zen, Bodhidharma. Unsurprisingly, it holds special import for meditators.

I would also like to explain why I am writing under a pseudonym. While the PhD is true, *Deshi*, the Japanese term for learner or religious novice, is not. I currently work for an organization (a school) which can legally dismiss me for my sexuality, hence the protection of a pseudonym. The need for secrecy as a self-protective measure is a regrettable but all too common fact for gay people, and illustrates our forced invisibility in an era of unjust legal sanctions.

What I can openly say is that this book is about hope — hope that it is truly possible for us to make a better world for ourselves step by step right here in the midst of so much suffering. My journey of the last ten years is in the following pages. May those who suffer find encouragement and hope within.

What Gay People Bring to Practice

In the year 2000 I came out. I am not going to go into the details, suffice it to say that this turned my daily life upside down. I had always been taught that if I obeyed the laws, paid my taxes and worked hard, the system would do the right thing by me. The equation was simple. If you're not doing anything illegal, you can't be treated like a criminal. If you are treated unfairly, you turn to the law. It was with profound disillusionment that I realized this no longer applied to me. A kiss could now lose me my job. In fact, the government happily discriminated against me — it actually sought me out on purpose. While I knew this happened to other people, I never thought it would happen to me.

It is a very bitter thing indeed to learn of your own naivety. When the privileges I enjoyed as a heterosexual were taken away, I fell hard. Although it was liberating at first, it soon turned into the realization that I'd gone from top of the food chain to 'pond scum,' 'weirdo,' 'pedophile' or, if the early morning religious shows were to be believed, 'abomination.' I was no longer just me, I was 'gay.' This left me with dread and fear. And sometimes self-loathing.

Not surprisingly, I began to have panic attacks. We often say that we feel 'panicky' or 'anxious' but it wasn't until I had my first attack that I knew the real meaning of those words. I literally felt I could not breathe. I thought I was going to die. This was exacerbated by the breakup of a relationship. Since I would be jobless if anyone found out, for several months I had to cry in the toilets in between teaching classes. It was a shocking first step.

Providentially, a turning point came in the form of The Spitting Man. The Spitting Man was a huge hulk of a man I once worked with. As a severe homophobe and intense evangelical Christian, anti-gay comments were fast and frequent whenever anyone ventured near the topic of homosexuality. To give you an idea of his personality, for some inexplicable reason he bailed me up one day with a quick joke — 'How can you tell a homo has been in a bar before you? You see the stool he left behind.' He laughed and left. I felt hijacked, like a truck had run over me. There wasn't even time to comment, although I have no idea what I would have said. After that, I literally felt ill whenever he came near me.

One day someone or something made him angry. We were sitting around the lunch table at work. Since I was sitting next to him, he stood up and leaned over me, talking very heatedly about the fact that God did not mean orifices to be used in the way homosexuals use them. He was so worked up the spittle was flying from his mouth. It was then that I lost my hearing. Everything slowed down and my voice in my head said, 'We are exactly the same.'

I didn't mean this in any mystical or transcendental sense. It was prior to kensho[3] and was a purely intellectual statement. I hated him and he hated me. I was a bigot about bigots. It was a horrible turn of events. I saw he suffered and that I did too! I was no better than he. In fact, it was even worse — I was exactly the same. The logic was undeniable.

As the spittle continued to issue forth from the corners of his mouth, I felt my entire being turn away and my hands open as if dropping bags out of them. There was an overwhelming sense of 'I

---

[3] A term for an enlightenment experience.

will not do this. This is not the way.' It was not a rejection but a turning to face once and for all my complete denial of feeling trapped. Change had to happen and I'd just seen the first signpost. It was around this time that I began to sit with a Zen group. My journey had begun.

Trapped Under the Radar

Suffering is universal. All people suffer. There are no exceptions. In this sense there is absolutely nothing unique or special about the suffering of gay people. Yet it is also true that particular groups have particular experiences which differ in certain ways from those of other groups. It is within these different backgrounds that groups formulate the view of the world with which they approach practice. The positive contributions gay people make to any *sangha*, and to an understanding of the Dharma, spring forth from lives of strength and optimism.

Yet it is imperative that recognition be given to the fact that common to all gay people is the particular suffering which comes from being homosexual. Our story is multi-faceted and includes both positive and negative aspects specific to our sexuality. Just as an appreciation of being black helps immensely in providing the support and understanding essential to building a strong community for African-Americans, so too is it helpful for *sanghas* to develop an understanding of the experiences of gay people if strong community is to be created.

For example, many gay practitioners bring to practice a sense of being under the radar, that our situation and suffering is invisible. To be gay often means feeling trapped. The coming out event illustrates this well. In the beginning coming out can be galling and frightening. I lost almost all of my friends and shut my mouth pretty quickly after that. It was only until three years had passed that I dared to again tell people, and for the most part, the response has been very compassionate. People listen intently and offer support.

At the same time however, there can often be a degree of disbelief or misunderstanding about how under the radar we can be. Sometimes it is a shock to heterosexuals because they sincerely and honestly think we live with the same opportunities or have exactly the same life. Often it is a shock simply because they have never given much thought to such a thing. At other times we are shut down or told point blank that when we talk about our difficulties we are creating fanciful and exaggerated fictions.

The Australian culture views complaints and complainers in a very negative light. To be thought of as a 'whinger' is to be seen as precious and painful. On the positive side, this has resulted in a history of self-reliance and a do-it-yourself mentality. The 'little Aussie battler,' the underdog who quietly makes good, is mythologized in this country. Yet this has also created the perception that to point out difficulty is to exaggerate. On a cultural level this general backdrop sometimes tends to inhibit frank discussion, and the gay person is both simultaneously visible and hidden. Many of us tough it out in silence.

The bottom line for most people in this world is to be happy and secure. For gay people this means searching for ways to be ourselves in a world which is often inimical to us. There are times, for example, that I really dislike being alive at this time in history. I can see equality on the horizon but my youth will have gone. I want to be free. Why couldn't I have been born in the future? Or better yet, in a socially liberal country. Conversely, I am thankful that I wasn't born 50 years ago when I could have been put in prison or lobotomized or placed in a sanatorium. Either way these kinds of thoughts represent dissatisfaction with being in the here and now. The present just doesn't measure up. This is not a good place to be and is certainly not conducive to spiritual awakening.

When I was about fourteen I saw a documentary on the original Stonewall activists. One of them said very bitterly, 'We just want what you have.' It has stayed with me ever since because he was so vehement and intense. I now know why. The present sucks for many gay people. There are many times we just don't want to be in our skins. This came to mind when I watched the movie *X Men: The Last Stand* in which a 'cure' had been found for the 'illness' of 'mutation.' The mutants were offered the chance to take a free injection and become 'normal' like non-mutants. Interestingly, when one of the main characters came out as a mutant to his parents, they asked whether it was just a phase. Sound familiar?

The ethical issue of course was that there was no sickness to cure, but since the mutants' suffering was so painful, their choice to take the injection was understandable. Given the chance to become straight and without the daily hassle of being 'different,' how many gay people would take it? I'm sure some of us would. Just the pure anonymity would be tempting. I cannot remember what it was like to walk down the street holding hands without receiving negative looks or risking my job. The unfortunate fact is that while many heterosexuals are more knowledgeable about homosexuality than ever before, many are also ignorant of the difference being gay makes on the street. It is below the level of their attention.

There are a variety of perfectly correct theories and facts about institutional structures and attitudes which enable this, but which the average person does not consciously participate in. It is also apparent that some heterosexuals do consciously perpetuate inequality. Whatever the case, some members of dominant groups may not see suffering in non-dominant groups or even their role in maintaining it. The simple fact is that we don't know what we don't know. The gay practitioner is often aware of this possibility when they first start Buddhist practice.

What don't some heterosexuals know? Currently there are 76 countries in which homosexuality is a crime punishable by a prison sentence and 5 countries in which it is punishable by death. In some countries lesbians are raped as a cure. This occurs even in places where same-sex marriage is legal. South African lesbians, for example, are subject to high rates of curative rape. The itinerary for my world trip won't include countries like these.

On a brighter note, in my country we are now three quarters the legal equivalent of de-facto heterosexuals. Having said that, we cannot marry, be openly gay at religious workplaces or enjoy many of the tax breaks given to married couples. In some Australian states we cannot have sex at the same legal age as heterosexuals nor adopt children. In many countries we have little or no rights at all. This has been decided for gay people in parliaments and congresses without our consent. It is common to feel that we have very little power to effect change unless the majority decides to support us.

It is not an exaggeration to say that there is nowhere we can go on this planet where we can expect to be the social equal in every way to a heterosexual, and where we can enjoy the same automaticity of approval and power. Many of us still have to watch every word, hide every kiss and monitor every action lest we be discovered. Many of us risk violence if we are openly gay in public. This is not limited to non-western countries. In fact, Mardi Gras events, the very occasions vaunted as examples of sexual freedom in the West, are also the days on which some of the highest rates of gay bashing occur. I still can't believe that some people would actually kill me. Me — some ordinary person from the suburbs. A poem I wrote reflects the fear I felt in the first year of coming out.

Realization (for the Newly Out)

Gradually,
what begins with
a creeping motion
gains momentum,
the subconsciously stored
piles up on itself,
and in an accumulative fashion
a concrete mass begins.
You notice things,
little things with big effects,
that you savor
quotes from
Gandhi,
Buddha,
Christ.
Strangely,
protest songs from the 60s
somehow seem relevant,
you start to look at *every* person,
listen for *every* word,
books by Nelson Mandela
are held up,
See! See!
He thinks we're OK!,

you divide the world into
'Who Would' and 'Who Wouldn't'
stick by you if they knew,
all of a sudden remote laws and legalities
actually matter in your daily life,
are essential to basic freedoms,
paranoia grows over the
difference of degree
between mouthing off
and rounding us up,
and you wake up one day
with the horrible realization
that you're the new nigger on the block,
the new Jew,
that your life is not safe,
not fair,
not recognized,
not trusted,
not supported,
and most of all
not
what
you
ever
thought
your situation
would be.

My poem did not seek to take away from the immense suffering
African-Americans and Jews have endured for centuries (and
continue to endure). Nor was it intending to say that we have the
same journey or that we have suffered more or less than these
people. I guess after coming out I began to feel real empathy with
those who have been forced to occupy the lowest positions. I felt
this because I realized I was now one of them. My dreams (such as
marriage) were now really just that — dreams. It was a complete
paradigm shift in the way I saw the world and myself.

Despite huge strides forward in equality, a feeling of being not only
invisible but forcibly trapped is endemic to the gay community
world-wide. This increases any feelings of insecurity we may

already have and exacerbates victim-complexes and paranoia. Plainly put, being invisible and trapped hurts and humiliates. For many gay people there is a sense of being stuck — of being at the whim of society and at the mercy of those more powerful than us.

When Barack Obama became President many African-Americans were ecstatic that they had lived long enough to see a black man achieve this. The concrete manifestation of change and possibility was almost too wonderful to bear. This reflects a history of buried hope and entrenched societal barriers; the fear that dreams cannot become reality if the system will not allow it. It reflects the nagging frustration that the current situation has no potential for change. In other words, regardless of our talents, morality or good works, we are born into this and we will die in it. Powerless inertia kills hope. This is, I suspect, the subconscious fear of many gay people.

It is true that we are visible more than ever and that most people have some kind of idea that we can experience discrimination. We have made huge strides in equal rights over the last decade and are now accepted in many circles. The situation in many countries is rapidly changing for the better. Yet there is still little public awareness in terms of the difference that being gay makes in daily life, and what affect that has upon our well-being. The last ten years has taught me that at this point in history many heterosexuals either don't know this, don't care or actively support the status quo. This bears direct relationship to our Buddhist practice.

So, what then is the solution? What sorts of things can we take into account when practicing as gay people? The following chapters outline different aspects a gay person may like to consider in order to practice beneficially. The Buddha said that the Dharma is verifiable and that each of us can come to know it for ourselves. In the same manner, I invite you to consider these aspects as you follow the Path.

2
Recognition and Acceptance

As a Buddhist I know that ignorance of reality causes suffering but that if someone really sees reality, suffering can end. The suffering of gay people is a reality, and the idea that this cannot be changed is folly. Recognition of this can be facilitated by education and through giving voice to our experiences. This can be done at both an individual level and at an institutional level by *sangha* leaders. The current difficulty with raising awareness is that the onus of instruction is usually upon the gay person. After all, no one knows what they don't know.

Have you ever noticed that after you learn a new word, suddenly you hear it everywhere or that after a break up the radio stations only ever seem to play love songs? This is because our conscious attention has been drawn to something which previously passed unnoticed. Yet from my own practice I know that it becomes easier when things are made clearer and more personal by placing them within a framework that other people can relate to. This is an area in which *Sangha* leaders can foster institutional support, and the fear of the separate and mysterious 'other' can be transmuted into mutual fellowship. There are several ways this can be done.

To help this process along, *Sangha*s must recognize that even though the law may in some cases hamper any effort to make practice places totally safe, it is of paramount importance to attempt it anyway. For example, since I work in a religious organization which enjoys certain exemptions from National Discrimination Laws, everyone who enters the *zendo*[4] is a threat to me.

There are only two places I can truly be me — at home and in my *zendo*. It is vital to my spiritual and mental well-being to keep the *zendo* a safe place, but even there I have to trust the universe if I wish to continue on the Path. The fact is that if I want to enjoy

---

[4] Zendo — meditation hall.

community and access to a teacher, I have to maintain practice with other people. Everyone in my *Sangha* is aware that I'm gay and is fine with it. I would rather the *zendo* be a place where I can totally be me than a place of censorship, so rather than ask them never to mention my sexuality, I entrust them with the information and with a sense of timing and discernment. This sometimes hasn't gone to plan.

Once at a retreat with another group someone opened a conversation about gay people and directed it to me. As it turned out, another participant (not from my *zendo*) had just gone skiing with my boss! I discussed it with a teacher who cleverly came up with the solution of asking this person not to mention me because Buddhist meditation might cause a problem for my Christian employer. What a relief. The bottom line is that I have to trust the universe because if something inadvertently gets back to my workplace, I will be called into the Principal's office to explain. I will have to look at that person and lie to their face. That's the reality for me if I want to keep the job I love. That's the reality for many gay people in religious organizations.

Uncertainty about whether to come out to the *Sangha* may also feature in the gay practitioner's life. We all know someone or have been that person who has lost something after coming out — friends, social position, a religious community. The fact is, despite positive advancements over the last ten years, we often don't get that promotion, endorsement or job if we come out. Many of us have been kicked out of our families and fear we will be shunned.

Despite all this, many Buddhist communities in the West regard gay people in a positive light. At the same time, communities need to understand that that doesn't necessarily convince us coming out will be in our favor. This is not personal at all. From experience I know that just because people say they are accepting doesn't mean they actually are.

I can never predict how people will react to me being gay. People who seem accepting are actually not and vice versa. Some people are theoretically in support of equal rights but don't want to mix with us. Others have no referent point for how to interact with us. Even terminology presents a problem — are partners called 'wives,' 'husbands' — what words are used with gay people? The sense of unease can be palpable. Some would prefer us to be 'less gay' (whatever that means). Instead of being a place of ease, the meditation hall has the potential to be yet another uncomfortable place to squirm. Quite frankly, sometimes it's just easier to keep quiet.

All of this probably does not occur to many heterosexual Dharma brothers and sisters purely because it is not their experience. For a peaceful heart-mind to be developed, gay people need to accept this with magnanimity. While it is perfectly legitimate for us to feel angry about any lack of recognition or interest in our welfare, this is only half the story, and it is unfair not to see the whole picture.

Undoubtedly, we all want to be loved and when we feel we are not it is painful. Not surprisingly, this often dominates the cultural products of marginalized groups. In singing about the pain of being black and poor, for example, many of Jamaica's reggae stars sing about the lack of love they feel from their own countrymen and women. Anyone who listens to this music cannot fail to discern the pain of rejection and the undeniable sorrow in their voices. How terrible it is for people to feel separation and isolation.

In a perfect world, no one lives in a bubble and everyone pursues new and different ideas and experiences. In a perfect world, we enlighten ourselves about what we don't know. The fact is however, that much of the time we attend to what matters to us. What doesn't affect us is not seen or cared about. This truth stands for everyone — gay or straight — there are no exceptions. As much as I feel the legitimacy of my hurt, I feel the rightness of not punishing people for what I also have done and still do. When I intellectualize this, my head hurts. It is only through sincere and long-term practice that the reconciliation of these two truths has been made possible.

Communities can also recognize that it is important to either refrain from or approach with sensitivity any theorizing in a Buddhistic sense about people's gayness or straightness. Many of us have encountered pronouncements upon the nature or transience of our sexuality. There are a number of variations on this theme — it's a choice, it's a phase, it's too much soy while in the womb, it's a reversible 'conversion.' In the Buddhist world there are all sorts of Dharmic explanations for why we are like we are. These can trap us if we buy into their concepts as absolute reality.

Gender attributes is a good example. Even if not anti-homosexual per se, traditional doctrine can tend to silence or marginalize any interpretation not heterosexual purely as a by-product of the assumption that male-female is the norm, or because sacred texts have been written for and by heterosexual men. Depending on one's views, traditional doctrine can be liberating, but at other times can also act as a limiting filter. This becomes apparent in some of the ways in which Western *sanghas* have sought to apply traditional doctrine to modern issues.

Some have suggested, for example, that homosexuality is not inherently evil but the result of cause and effect. That is, if a concurrent number of past lives were of one gender, that dominant gender's inclinations pass on regardless of whether the current recipient is the same gender or not. The result is same-sex attraction because multiple rebirths as one gender heavily conditions sexual karma. According to this interpretation, if we have been born a man in successive lifetimes and are now a woman, we will acquire the inclinations of a male. It is for this reason that women love women, and men love men.

For many this is a comfort since it makes clear we are not intrinsically evil. A great many gay Buddhists feel gratitude at this. Karma is something anyone can work on, and an awareness of karma can help us shape our intentions positively. This is good news. Yet there may also be those who find the connection between sexuality and karma to be too attached to fixed ideas of gender to be valid. That is, ideas about what a man or woman 'is' or 'isn't.' Instead of accepting that women can love women in their own right, it is solely interpreted through the lens of one gender — as 'male' karma.

This rests on the inviolate assumption that only men can truly love women because this is an eternally male-owned characteristic. According to some Buddhists, then, it appears that everything in the Universe is impermanent but gender-owned attraction. In my case, I find it far more beneficial to sit with the *Diamond Sutra,* which makes clear that although women appear as 'women,' essentially speaking they are not. In fact, gender does not exist in a reality where ultimately there are no separate objects. This is why the Buddha said that in all things there is neither male nor female.

Sitting with this counters my tendency to cling to gender and permanent, unchanging ownership of certain characteristics. It may also be that rebirth does not sit well with many secular Buddhists. Others may find that they become caught up in numbers — how many consecutive lifetimes are needed for gender-centric karma to form? Since gay people are in the minority, does this mean that only a few people have this type of karmic background? Conversely, some of us may be of the opinion that our own egos prevent us from accommodating the above and that we are trapped by the 'weeds' of our own concepts. These prevent us from accepting the truth.

Whatever the view, the temptation is for doctrinal theorizing to become mired in concepts and bean-counting. If we are to inquire into the *koan* of *'what is this?'* it is inevitable that we cannot escape encountering all sorts of interpretations. Gay practitioners may take a strictly traditional line on their sexuality or find new angles on old ideas. The efficacy of any approach varies from person to person. My advice would be not to bring theories up if they are not mentioned first. Sensitivity is a must and a sense of timing essential.

Also, if there is any difficulty in having gay people in the *sangha*, it is imperative that teachers and leaders address it. *Sangha* leaders must sit with whether they will or won't be comfortable with a gay practitioner. This does not mean acceptance of homophobia. Negativity and discrimination still occur, but the days when they were automatically accepted are over. It is fairly difficult in the West nowadays for homophobia to be neatly swept under the carpet and the evidence erased. The 'gay problem' will continue to present itself again and again until society, and that includes the Buddhist community, deals with it once and for all. This will vary from community to community, and will even differ according to personalities. There are many variables.

Teachers also need to keep an eye on any hostility or discomfort which may occur, and take appropriate measures for the peaceful integration and protection of gay practitioners. There may be no problem at all, or that if there is, things smooth over by themselves with time. If need be however, teachers can take relevant people aside and discuss their reservations sensitively and privately. They can encourage gay practitioners to bring partners to communal activities or give Dharma talks in which acceptance and tolerance are highlighted. It is only natural that some people will be ill at ease if they have never had the opportunity to talk with us.

If things come to a head, it may also be of benefit to openly discuss any concerns with the whole *sangha*. The sexual scandals in the Western Buddhist Community in the 1980s and 90s highlighted the need for active listening and for looking issues in the eye and dealing with them. Whatever the case, if things do not improve, it is no good ignoring the tension. Gay people are particularly adept at sensing this — we've had to as a protective measure.

Conversely, if there is no difficulty in having gay people in a *sangha* it is a good idea to be upfront about that too. Any advertisement of that fact is a plus. The perception that every gay person will experience problems in joining a community is incorrect. It is very encouraging to see that many groups have incorporated sexuality into their Welcome/Mission Statement. This provides huge encouragement in making that first step to the *sangha*.

My own experience was super positive. In so many ways the Patriarchs and Matriarchs of Buddhism did not deceive me and neither did my teacher. Despite not having any reservations about homophobia in my Zen community I still waited about two years before telling the *Roshi*.[5] I just wasn't ready. When I finally did she listened intently but barely moved an eyebrow. She nodded and said, 'Ok.' It was as if I had said 'I'm wearing a black t-shirt.' How natural. She assured me that the Dharma[6] is not separate to my sexuality and that I am not excluded from it because of my sexuality. It was made absolutely clear that there were no reservations at all. I nearly cried with relief. My *Roshi* was still going to be my teacher even though she knew the truth. It was a complete

---

[5] *Roshi* — the person who gives spiritual and religious guidance to a Zen sangha.

[6] In this sense, the Dharma refers not to religious doctrine but to reality. This is an additional meaning of the term

non-issue. It was also made clear that should anyone in the *sangha* express negativity, she would discuss it with them. All these things made me feel protected and welcomed.

It is understandable how all sorts of worries might play with the minds of many gay people. The disenchanfrisement of certain segments of society results in profound disillusionment, isolation, bitterness and fear. It's tempting to feel that no one can understand what it is like to be gay or straight or married or black or Asian — the list goes on. Yet while it is true that we will never know what it is to be anyone other than ourselves, we can all come to an understanding in our own way.

I do not agree with the statement that a straight person will never know what it's like to be gay. My straight friends and I have been in the process of educating each other for many years about how straight and gay people live. As with all things this has taken time and there have been occasional hiccups, but they have a perfectly workable and fine understanding of my experience.

There seems to be a sense of ego or a victim mentality whenever anyone says, 'You don't know what it is like to be *x*,' not to mention a futile attempt to hang on to what is essentially impermanent and empty.[7] This phrase is used as a kind of automatic disclaimer and its function is the privileging of knowledge. It shuts out anyone's claim to understanding purely on the grounds that they do not have the exact same experience as others. It's as if someone is automatically rendered deaf, dumb and blind (and therefore, incapable of making a logical observation) purely because they have never done what others have. This is just not realistic. While some people do lack the empathy and knowledge needed to walk in another person's shoes, this denies the fact that many of us have the hearts and minds to truly understand another person.

If it was true in every sense that no one could ever understand what it is like to be another person, the world would stop. Carried to its logical conclusion, no one would connect with anyone. Being short, I couldn't truly connect with tall people because I will never come

---

[7] Empty — that nothing possesses a permanent and separate identity because everything is connected and changing. It does not mean nothingness

to know what tallness is. I couldn't talk to person A because they have a different skin color, and I wouldn't bother meeting Person B because they listen to country music and I'm a classical fan.

There will always be those who reject and those who do not listen, but it is entirely possible for gay and straight people to be separately one. We are all equipped with hearts and minds which can develop empathy and understanding for another person in our own way. As we come to know and embody the Dharma, we also realize that we are not just capable of intellectually and empathically understanding others, we are others. This 'at-one-ness' is the ultimate connectivity.

As the Buddha said in the *Sutta Nipata* of the *Pali Canon*:

> *As I am, so are others; as others are, so am I.*
> *Having thus identified self and others, harm*
> *no one nor have them harmed.*

I understand in my own way what it is like to be another person, and that understanding can be perfectly adequate. Education and recognition are the keys. Given that certain things need to occur in order to optimize the experience of gay people within a *sangha* however, the choice of whether to practice with or separately from heterosexuals can be an interesting one.

3
Practicing Together or Apart

When it comes to choosing a group to sit with, we can practice with or separately from heterosexuals. To my knowledge a discussion within the gay community about this has not occurred to the same extent that it has within African-American and ethnic Buddhist communities. Yet we can make reasonable summations about how and why people make their choices. In terms of choosing gay-only *sanghas*, there are a number of factors which may dissuade the practitioner from sitting with other types of groups.

It is not known, for example, how many gay people exist in Buddhist communities in the West since one cannot definitively tell who is gay unless they are openly out. Yet it is reasonable to expect that the proportion of gay people to straight people will mirror the wider population. This means that gay people will be in lesser numbers and may in some cases be the only gay person in the *sangha*. From my own experience this appears to be true.

*Sangha*s also reflect the social and political structure of the wider society. Gay people may not be in leadership positions or fellow *sangha* members may frown upon homosexuality. Gay people might not feel welcome or supported because they do not fit dominant patterns, and it may be that straight people are unaware of the subtle and unseen ways in which they enact this power structure.

The Buddhist community in the West is also overwhelmingly homogeneous in that it consists largely of upper-middle-class white people. This can be of concern to those of other races, but might also be dissuasive to white gay people in its 'mainstream, heterosexual' ways of viewing and dealing with the world. All of these can make for a difficult time not only in coming out, but in creating a sense of ease and normality within a *sangha*. In essence, some people would rather practice within an atmosphere of similarity than difference, since the latter may interfere with the mind state of sitters and trigger feelings of fear and separation.

The case for practicing separately is based upon the recognition that different groups have different needs, and these may be met more efficiently by having separate spaces for different affinity groups. Those who prefer separate groups view this as creating a safer and more suitable place to explore issues related to identity and discrimination. The pain and pressure of being in a sexual minority can be alleviated by practicing within an accepting and supportive environment. In safe places people feel freer to ask questions and explore issues.

It goes without saying that there is great psychological benefit in being openly gay. Yet we come under tremendous pressure from society to be circumspect about our sexuality. As a result, some of us are extremely careful in our speech and mannerisms in order to manage 'signs' of gayness. For example, we may avoid using the pronoun 'we' when referring to our partner or use alternative terms such as 'roommate' so as to minimize suspicion. This entails compartmentalizing our lives so that we appear differently to different sets of people. Such a way of conducting oneself can be extremely tiring and frustrating, not to mention internally dissociative at times. Knowing that it need not be this way and that dominant groups enforce this behavior only adds to the frustration.

For these reasons, it may be that sitting with those who have had similar experiences is a more expedient way of facilitating any healing process. Gay-only groups can aid self-development in a way which is suited to the target audience and informed through first-hand experience. Some heterosexual people may feel guilty or defensive when the subjects of homosexuality and homophobia are brought up, while gay people can resent having to tell yet another person about their story. As I said earlier, sometimes it's easier just to keep quiet.

Practicing with like people can also be an important step in helping retreats in general become more inclusive. As more gay people take up the Buddhist Path, they may feel more comfortable attending retreats which include non-gay people. Buddhism is new to the West and can be strange and daunting to the newcomer, let alone with the added worry of practicing with those who may make the experience feel less safe. Seeing gay people in leadership positions is inspiring and uplifting. It is a boost of confidence which helps us feel strong enough to function positively in society. A sense of empowerment is important for any marginalized group. We need to know that we can hold our own. This is not necessarily a rejection of straight *sanghas* but a need to practice within a particular environment. Some also argue that one way is not better than the other, it's just different.

Needless to say, safety, support, understanding, ease of practice, specific programs and inclusive leadership may be found within any *sangha*. It is an error to think that *sanghas* not specifically for one group will automatically mirror societal attitudes or cannot cater for a variety of practitioners. In my own *sangha* I cannot imagine any circumstance in which I would be denied something on the basis of my sexuality. While some of my fellow sitters are not aware of my experiences and outlook, they express a willingness to reach out to me whenever I express discomfort about anything. Their compassion overrides any lack of information or experience. They are willing to work with anyone who enters the *sangha*. I have personally learnt a great deal from watching how the teachers have approached and cared for different people. They impress me with their flexibility and kindness.

Some gay people might also feel that to separate people into categorical groups will create disharmony, a sense of inequality or exclusiveness, and enhance unskillful habits of mind which focus on difference rather than sameness. Categorizing can prevent us from learning to relate to other groups in society outside of those within which we place ourselves. The presence of gay people within *sanghas* is a reminder that society consists of many diverse groups, and interaction with gay people is educating society to that fact.

To make the *sangha* holistic, many also feel that it needs to be inclusive rather than exclusive in its daily practice. Diversity needs to be more than a concept. Those in favor of practicing with heterosexuals draw support for diversity and inclusiveness from the Buddhist doctrine of interdependent origination.[8] Since we are all ultimately connected, many feel that this should be reflected conventionally in the way we conduct our behavior. While a free society guarantees that we have the right to practice separately, mutuality is not reflected in the separation of groups according to cultural, racial, sexual or economic factors. This contradiction can cause conflict within ourselves and our communities, not to mention our nations. It may increase a feeling of separation rather than connection.

Lastly, the choice of whether or not to practice with non-gay people may also be a simple one. That is, that gay-only groups simply do not exist in abundance. Accessing a Buddhist group in itself is not always possible, even in a big city, let alone a group consisting solely of gay people. In my country, the Google search terms *gay dharma, LGBT dharma, gay sangha, gay Buddhists, gay Zen, queer sangha, lesbian sangha* draw only a few hits. There is little advertising and few groups just for gay people.

Whatever the case, it is important to keep in mind two considerations — compassion and clear seeing. It is obvious that the clear seeing of reality can occur in any setting and any *sangha*. There is no other place to realize than where you are. Every place is the place to wake up. This means that even though we may be the only gay person in a *sangha*, it does not take anything away from the fact that we all have the potential for realization. The sticking point for many people is most probably the setting in which that realization is fostered. The degree to which the environment promotes or interferes with practice is an important factor to consider.

As a school teacher this reminds me of the issue of home schooling. Some parents feel they can provide an education which is more tailored to their child's specific needs than mainstream systems can. While I personally do not favor that option, if my child was being bullied or humiliated to the extent that they would suffer more if they went to school, I would not hesitate to home school them. They

---

[8] Interdependent origination — the law of causality. All phenomena lack independent, permanent, or absolute existence. Everything is interconnected, dependent on something else and in a continual process of transformation.

would be placed in a setting where they could learn and feel safe. It is not worth the mental health of a child to force the other option on them. This would especially be the case if the leadership of the institution did not put certain measures in place to protect and nurture my child, and censure the bully. This would also mean that I could specifically tailor any program to my child's needs.

At the same time however, I would recognize that there are limitations to any system, and home schooling restricts the type of interaction one has and with whom. It may train students to learn in one way and not another. It may open students up to one way of thinking but not others. Whatever the choice, compassion needs to be at the forefront of our minds. It is no good forcing ourselves to practice with straight people if this brings distress and fear. At the risk of fence-sitting, a case by case basis seems the best way to go.

A close friend of mine sometimes feels the need to say 'get over yourself' whenever I am being somewhat precious. I take this quite well and her intention is only ever good. She is almost always right on the mark. In the *Digha Nikaya* of the *Pali Canon*, the earliest written scriptures of Buddhism, the Buddha said that it is by education that some ideas arise and by education again that others pass away. Regardless of whether we practice with or separately from heterosexuals, the task then is for each of us to educate and release our own hearts — to get over ourselves. One way to do this is to take a panoramic look at things.

4
Categorical, Panoramic and Beyond

It is natural that we all seek to clarify who and what we are. Definitions and theories can provide structures by which we clearly look at what is in front of us. There is absolutely nothing wrong with categorizing, defining and specifying. To act we must know what it is that we are dealing with. Solutions can only be found when problems are identified. Yet when this is done without the benefit of a wide perspective we can buy into our concepts as absolute and total reality.

This is not a skilful view because we can come to relate more to our conception of something than the thing itself. In this way we enslave ourselves and create the very prison we seek escape from. Without a balance, we cannot overcome our own limitations and be happy — we cannot get over ourselves. Of course, as anyone who has meditated knows, this is much easier said than done.

It can be difficult to know who we are. To determine parameters, the difference between ourselves and others must be identified. It is no use denying that there are differences — there are. Yet herein lies the trap — definitions mark boundaries and boundaries separate people. Separation is a fact but it is also a non-fact. On a daily-life, surface level we are separate beings but on an essential level there are no separations at all. The attainment of this kind of panoramic understanding of reality is absolutely necessary for a peaceful heart-mind.

This does not mean that we must have years of practice under our belts or enlightenment experiences to understand this. Benefit can come immediately from even just an intellectual recognition, from making it clear in our own heads. Reading, listening and being curious about both self and others goes a long way to finding a liberating equilibrium.

In Buddhism this equilibrium is said to be achieved when one recognizes that phenomenal, conventional, daily-life categories are only part of the story — by themselves they do not represent the *totality* of reality. When the great masters speak, they speak from a holistic and intuitive understanding — they have width, breadth and depth. A partial view blinds us to the whole and allows us to be content with not knowing what we don't know. As the Buddha said in the *Digha Nikaya:*

> *That people are unknowing doesn't mean that*
> *they are unknowing like cows or goats. Even*
> *ignorant people look for a pathway to reality.*
> *But in searching for it they often misunderstand*
> *what they encounter. They pursue names,*
> *categories and labels instead of going beyond*
> *names to that which is real.*[9]

When we reside only in particulars we remain ignorant about the larger picture. It is this larger picture which helps release us from the confines of our own ego and suffering.

Race is an excellent example of this. On one level race is an ever present reality. Prejudice based on that reality has devastatingly real effects. Race has meant one people thrived and another were put in the holds of ships and wrenched from their loved ones. So on one hand, race is a completely true fact, yet on another level, a complete fiction. It is a social construct. As an evolutionary and biological concept, race did not exist prior to the seventeenth century.

The color of a person's skin exists, but we made up the idea that we can categorize the whole person in relation to that one thing. Judging all of a person by one feature is irrational, not to mention unfair. If this was totally accurate, it would be equally reliable to separate us into inferior and superior groups according to eye color, the size of our little toe or the roughness of the skin on our elbows. Yet, at some point, the color of someone's skin was made the pivot

---

[9] From *The Buddha Speaks*, edited by Anne Bancroft, ©2000 by Anne Bancroft. Reprinted by arrangement with Shambhala Publications Inc., Boston, MA.

point by which you could tell intelligence, ability and nature — by which you could ascertain who and what a person was. As such, it became a way of ranking and dividing society into groups, and ensured some remained marginalized while others were empowered. In this way, 'race' became real.

This and other intellectual constructs may seem political, economic and social but they are also enlightenment issues as well. This is because the mind is a powerful thing. As the *Flower Ornament* and *Perfection of Wisdom* sutras tell us, all things of the world are created by Mind. Modern psychology also notes that we see what we want to see. In whatever way we choose to label the mind, whether 'little' (the intellect) or 'Big' (non-dual consciousness), it still remains that it can do anything. We can recognize it as boundlessly open like all else, or we can purposefully use it to foster the delusion of separation through dualistic and divisive frameworks placed on reality. It can be the mind of delusion, thusness or beyond.

There is consensus in the Scientific community that we all share universal genetic ancestors. In listing human sequences of DNA, the Human Genome project led scientists to discover that all modern humans share a common female ancestor who lived in Africa about 140,000 years ago, and all men share a common male ancestor who lived in Africa about 60,000 years ago. This means that we are related to all people of the world since we all emerged from the same ancestors in Africa. We *are* other 'races,' whatever the color of our skin may be.

In one sense, this also means that people who are racist are actually advocating hate against themselves, because while there is a biological foundation for our species, there is absolutely none for race. We are all members of the same hominid subspecies Homo sapiens. As such, race has no taxonomic significance. There is no scientific basis for it at all. It can either be bought into totally or recognized as a social construct which has a conventional meaning but not an essential one. I can imagine that this fact is not well received in certain quarters.

To be sure, we can make some perfectly accurate generalizations about groups of people. It's whether we see them through narrow and intractable lenses that's the problem. After all, a black man from the Congo shares some of the characteristics of a black man from LA. They both live in a world where they are black, and it is inevitable that this shapes commonality. But they may be very different at the same time. There might be other more reliable indicators of who they are such as culture, religion, personality and family. Even then, these indicators of identity aren't foolproof.

The social construction of identity applies to homosexuality as well. On one level it's entirely real. If it's not, who the heck doesn't have equal rights at the moment? At the same time, it's a social construct. Even the word 'homosexual' is only just over 100 years old. There was no such category before that. In fact, some people believe that the construct of homosexuality will disappear over time purely because it is a social construct. Ideas, classifications and rankings are as impermanent as everything else.

Both homosexuality and heterosexuality arose out of a particular time period and perception, and it may be reasonable to expect that the rigid distinctions these were built upon will one day disappear if their underlying perceptions change. That is, if sexuality comes to be seen as more fluid and inclusive, then perhaps current constructs will no longer function as the focal point for identity, and will no longer adequately apply to who and what a person is. Whether or not this actually occurs, it necessarily challenges the idea that sexual identity is permanent and lasting, an idea not unfriendly to the Buddhist concept of not-self.

Yet in this present age, it is very easy to know you're 'gay' because it often seems that the whole world is not. When we look around we don't see ourselves very much. Gay people aren't on billboards and aren't in ads on TV. If we want movies which have gay characters they're automatically classed as 'gay' movies and we have to go to a 'gay' DVD store. There are no 'straight' DVD stores by the way. There's no need for them — that movies are 'straight' is an unspoken assumption. The gay filter has also been applied to the history books in high schools so that the lives of gay people are absent. It's as though we have never existed.

In this way, heterosexuality can be overwhelming. It's often the only show in town. The sheer weight of its ubiquity holds us down at times. It hems us in and silences us. Yet we forget that even heterosexuality is a socially constructed category which is not solid in itself. It may be a category which indicates opposite sex attraction but in truth that's not even absolute because sexuality is fluid for some people. But it goes even deeper than that.

The *Diamond Sutra* states that essentially there is no gender but it could just as easily state, 'In all things there is neither heterosexual nor homosexual.' It is evident that both categories are not the total lynchpin of identification we've been told they are. Imagine if an alien appeared out of a UFO one day and asked you what heterosexuals were like. Do they like movies? *Yes*. What kinds? *All kinds*. Are they intelligent? *Some are, some are not*. What color are they? *All colors*. Where do they live? *Everywhere*. Are they moral? *Some are, some are not*. These are the same answers that could be given for homosexuals, or for people with a certain eye color or height. These answers carry the same limitations at indicating who and what people are. This is because we are more than our descriptors. Everything is more than its descriptor.

In fact, in focusing too intently on our gayness, the unintentional by-product is that we can actually reinforce the legitimacy of the constructs by which others judge us. That is, in focusing on how 'different' we are from heterosexuals, we actually strengthen the position of those who base their power on that difference. We legitimize heterosexuality because we have used it as a concrete comparison. Yet it too is a construct. This does not mean that we should pretend we are all the same or deny opposite-sex attraction. It means that we must be careful about buying into our concepts and constructs wholesale.

If we over-emphasize our differences or regard ourselves as special cases, we can box ourselves into a corner by overly focusing on sex and sexuality to the detriment of other aspects of our lives. We can stereotype ourselves into ways of acting and talking so that even gay people can reject other gay people if they aren't 'gay' enough. If we lose sight of our essential wholeness, a one-sided view is all we can see.

As time goes on I'm not sure what the concrete dimensions of gay are because I don't know what characteristics other than same-sex attraction would make me that different from a heterosexual. After all, I might have more in common with a heterosexual than another gay person. In fact, I would forget I was gay if I wasn't reminded so often of how supposedly 'different' or deviant this makes me. This does not mean that I don't consider myself gay. I do. But it is only one of many things about me. It's an important thing, but not the defining point.

When we are set apart from others, it is easy for us to define ourselves by whatever attribute is claimed to be the culprit. For this reason, it is easy for gay people to fall into the trap of thinking our gayness is all there is to us — that we are solely defined by that one characteristic. After all, this 'difference' is the cause of social sanctions. Some heterosexuals feel it necessary to protect children, the state of marriage and even Western civilization from homosexuality. This is why we cannot enjoy the same freedoms as others. Since some people make such a big deal out of it, we feel that it really must be a big deal. Our 'difference' can seem overwhelmingly important. And in one sense it is, but again, this is not the total story.

Obviously, while reality cannot be totally encapsulated by words, we cannot do without language. We need words to communicate and to explain what it means to be a gay person at this point in history. It is integral to being understood. Gay people have struggled with this at times but it is important for us to stand on our own two feet. Self-determination requires that we examine who we are. The sticking point is whether we fall into the inherent trap in all of this. That is, our categories often hold such sway over our minds that we can have a less than balanced or fair view.

Some activists, for example, might dismiss me as a co-oppressor for remaining in the closet at work. For some gay women I am not a 'true lesbian' because I have had sex with a man. Others can be less than friendly to butch and femme couples because they perceive them as perpetuating the same sorts of stereotypical rigidity found in the heterosexual world. Women who don't affect a certain fashion can be told they don't 'look gay.' I've been told that several times. Gay people have not come to a consensus even about what word to use to describe ourselves. Some dislike queer and dyke, while others feel this entirely appropriate. To some, the word gay only refers to men. Other people squirm when they hear the word 'homosexual' because it's clinical or like a flashback to 1950 newsreels in which police went out in search of 'deviants.'

Conversely, gay people have been subject to numerous categorizations by heterosexuals and our freedoms significantly curtailed as a result. The devastating effect of labeling homosexuality as a mental illness in the Diagnostic and Statistical Manual of Mental Disorders cannot be understated. It legitimized incarceration in sanatoriums and privileged one group over another. Thankfully, being gay is no longer officially listed in the mental health books in Western countries, but it did make concrete the idea that there is an automatic link between homosexuality and pedophilia. While this concept is fast becoming the discourse marker of the illogical and is usually speedily identified as the red flag of the bigot, it still rears its ugly head whenever talk of gay parenting and adoption arises.

Clearly, we need to keep an eye on how attached we are to our words and categories because they are never without underlying beliefs. As Frank Herbert, the famous science fiction writer, once pointed out, when we believe in certain words, we believe not only in their hidden arguments, but in the assumptions underpinning those arguments. Such assumptions can often be full of holes, but remain most precious to the convinced.

Our beliefs may be correct or incorrect. They may help improve the daily lives of people or contribute to a lack of understanding. I hope that both gay and straight people clearly see each other and remain open to a panoramic view, because our perceptions of each other can get in the way of true fellowship. An intention to really see allows us to sit with categories and concepts and to recognize the smoke and mirrors.

The Buddha pointed out that we are capable of making use of concepts and conventional terms without clinging to them. It is possible to honor our particular sexual identity without becoming attached to it. In other words, we can lead lives in which our categories do not set up a permanent gap between self and other. Ultimately we may come to see that there is neither self nor other in a universe which is One.

Of course, my Zen teacher is probably grimacing at this description because it is full of concepts and words. Practice is about moving beyond both the categorical and panoramic, but that's best left for teachers and adepts to explain. All I wish to do is to alert both gay and straight people to the fact that there is a larger picture, and when completely caught in our own little boxes, we miss it. This only increases our suffering. Boxes are useful but not if they restrict our view to just four walls. This is especially applicable to those of us who buy into the 'Who Suffers Most' argument. This is the apple every culture bites into and it only brings misery. For gay people it can taint our entire practice.

5
The Most Suffering, the Most Special

One day at work it struck me that almost everyone in the room was talking about how difficult their life was. All of us were trying very hard to convince the others that we suffered the most. As a species we seem to have a special predilection towards needing recognition of how worse off we are than others. Some of us can revel in receiving the Biggest Sufferer prize and it is tempting for minorities who experience pain and prejudice to develop this mentality.

This kind of thinking is mentioned in the *Sutta Nipata* which cautions us to avoid viewing ourselves as being either superior, inferior or equal to others. We are cautioned against this way of thinking because these are considered distinct modes of egocentricity. The first, superiority-conceit, is founded on a sense of privilege and arrogance originating from a feeling of superiority. It is based on the perception that 'I am better than others.' Equality conceit takes the form 'I am equal.' In modern society this can be seen in attachment to the idea that people similar to oneself are the only ones who really know how to treat others equally, or that only systems deemed 'egalitarian' can deliver good outcomes. Inferiority complexes, the sense that we are not as good as others, can manifest in modern society as 'my life is worse than.' In addition, conceit in Buddhism also carries with it a sense of stiffness and rigidity, so much so that this is reflected in the body in how one walks and talks.

Each of these represents a vested interest in our own status. The danger in each form of conceit is that they reinforce the false sense of self. This is because conceit is based on self-advertisement through the delusion of comparison. In this way, even though victim-conceit can take the form of self-loathing, poor self-concept and negative self-talk, it is a form of ego-affirmation because it is based on reinforcing a limited and self-centered assessment of self. In fact, thinking that we suffer more than everyone else is a form of pride because it emphasizes how special we are in our suffering.

The *Sutta Nipata* states unequivocally that thoughts of equality, inferiority, and superiority are not there in the one who is not moved by such measurements. Neither are they there in the one who is not dependent on the existence of others to contrast their own qualities or lack thereof. Holding these egocentric opinions brings us into conflict with others because separation and comparisons are founded upon attachment to self-constructed categories. These categories may contain truth but they are not the total truth. Whatever the nature of the conceit however, its basic quality is a compulsion or need for recognition through comparison.

Compulsion is the operative word here. In the case of inferiority-conceit this does not suggest rejecting compassion, fair treatment or recognition of minorities. It is not about ignoring that certain people are in fact, victimized. Neither is it about denying the hurt and anger we feel when that happens. What the *Sutta Nipata* is talking about is *attachment* to being a victim. When we cannot let go of the need for recognition of our pain and/or identity as a sufferer due to our minority status, we suffer from victim-conceit. It becomes less about the suffering and more about us.

This is putting a chain around our own legs and buying into what enslaves us. It is investing in the very thing which ties us to the cause of our suffering. This is like loving the fire which burns you. For sure, there are times when we are victimized, but taking on the *mentality* of a victim and then cultivating that, are extra steps we choose to make. They are not natural to the situation — they're add-ons. This is *owning* the identity of a victim. Taking on these sensibilities adds even more hurt to what is already there.

Shantideva's *A Guide to the Bodhisattva's Way of Life* notes that when they find a dying lizard, even small birds act as if they were mighty garudas, the sacred kite on which the Hindu god Vishnu rides. Yet when we see ourselves as victims, even little things overcome us. In this way we set ourselves up. Shantideva, an 8th century Indian Buddhist scholar at Nalanda University, pointed out that this view of ourselves can only ever be to our detriment. It prevents us from being selfless bodhisattvas[10] in our daily lives because it reinforces our sense of self, and that false and separate 'self' is not engaged in positive mental habits in the first place.

The *Poems of Early Buddhist Nuns* recounts the struggles and accomplishments of Buddhist women as they strive for nirvana. Many of them rejoice in the equanimity found despite personal suffering. In one poem the author pleads for us to weigh up the advantages of being consumed by our own story and of seeking that which does not hurt us. She asks very directly why we want imprisonment to self when the Ageless exists. 'Come,' she says, 'reach up and touch the goal where all distractions cease, where sense is stilled, where bliss dwells; win Nirvana, win that sure salvation which has no beyond.' Another author asks us to 'get free, as free as the Moon. From out the Dragon's jaws sail clear on high, wipe off the debts that hinder you.'

The tone of these poems is both one of common sense and jubilation. This is because the ultimate ground of being[11] does not die, does not contain grief or hate, presents no obstructions, and is without fear. Having found such peace, these women are puzzled as to why we give attention to what hurts us. They're asking us to see the panoramic and better option. They're asking us to put out the fire.

Sometimes however, we've bought into a pattern too deeply to see it. If we're hurting, it's hard to step back and see the bigger picture. In the first few years after coming out I lit the fire of victim conceit often, and repeatedly spent time after time burning with excruciating emotions. My particular form of this was replaying every event again and again in my mind the way it should have gone. In it I would be smart and sassy and pull out all manner of facts and figures to bedazzle whoever didn't recognize the hurtful, bigoted misinformation they were spouting. They would recognize I was right and they were wrong. They would feel bad about it and

---

[10] Bodhisattva — a person who dedicates his/her life to the welfare of other beings.

[11] Ground of being — another term for ultimate reality. The ground out of which everything is constantly arising.

see that I knew more than them. Of course I knew better. I suffered. In their privileged little world they didn't know what real suffering was!

Suffering due to my sexuality did hurt me, but somehow the righteousness with which I reacted to it often felt good. In my head I told myself that this was about educating bigots but the truth was that it was often more about my ego than changing the hearts and minds of others. It made me feel justified because I was the one who suffered the most and people would recognize that. I'd be right, they'd be wrong and they'd know it. Rather than feeling justified because the cause of equal rights is just, I developed egotistical habits of mind. Unskillful habits of mind are hard to break and cause us much suffering.

When I finally raised my head up out of my own self-centeredness I could see a most surprising thing. I had thought it was all about other people but in fact, this was my song to sing and I had better go about learning to do it more skillfully and fairly. We can gain recognition without fuelling it with the fires of conceit. Once I learned that the more immediate (and necessary) task at hand was changing my own heart-mind, my practice changed its course. It was far better to find that place where the burning fire of ' I suffer the most' has no footing. That place is without the kind of thinking which separates people into victim and winner.

This mentality is dualistic and parasitical since it cannot exist without a host and a parasite. That is, if we totally buy into seeing ourselves as the underdogs and others as perpetrators, we are parasitic on those we would like to overthrow. We rely on their prejudice and a state of iniquity. Yet when the situation changes, equal rights are achieved and the perpetrators unable to act legally and effectively, what do we do then? Who do we 'fight' then? When gay people finally become 'winners,' we will either be left bereft or turn our oppositional mentality on someone else or even ourselves and our community. As Frank Herbert also said — too long a parasite and you cannot exist without a host.

Of course when a minority wants to win equal rights there's nothing wrong with that. As with everything to do with the heart-mind however, winning can be a trap if we are not careful. As the

Buddha warned, winning produces hostility in the winner and anguish in the loser. It is far better for our peace of mind, he suggested, to set both winning and losing aside. This does not mean that we should sit back and accept inequality, ignorance and misinformation. It means that we need to clearly see the risk in fighting for equality. That is, we can get so caught up in the righteousness of the struggle that we become self-righteous. In other words, we can use the cause to separate not unite. The thrill of winning and beating the loser becomes the primary goal. Being the victor and crushing the loser motivates us. We *own* winning.

As neuroscientists now tell us, by consistently thinking in one way, we organically rewire our brain to encourage certain thoughts and feelings, and to reduce or slow others. In this way, we train and shape our minds. By training our minds to possess winning, it sets up an almost unbending Us versus Them mentality which is difficult to change even after we have seen the true nature of things. This is a disaster for anyone who wishes to find lasting peace because it's also an existential knot. In an ultimate sense, there aren't winners or losers, there's no one to even be that because there are no separate entities in a reality in which all is One.

Believing we are more special because of who we are is just as dangerous as victim-conceit. When we get caught up in superiority-conceit we make life difficult for people if they don't measure up. This can rob people of their dreams through social, economic and legal sanctions. A person with a certain characteristic makes the grade but another completely fails the test. We can even create degrees of specialness. Apartheid was a good example of re-orienting a society into special and non-special groups. The separation of South Africans into Whites, Coloreds and Bantus during this era represents this idea in the extreme. Whole groups can be marginalized for not meeting a set of standards — they don't have the right clothes, education, papers, language, class, color or sexuality.

In 2004 the then Australian Prime Minister, John Howard, amended the Marriage Act to prevent same-sex marriage. In the Australian Constitution marriage is now seen as the lifelong union of a man and a woman to the exclusion of all others. In effect, this made the institution of marriage a special and exclusive club by denying gay people entry. Now retired Australian Greens Senator, Bob Brown, himself gay, referred to the legislation as hateful, and that this country now had a 'straight Australia policy.' This was in reference to another discriminative piece of legislation, the White Australia Policy, which was in place until the 1960s. This policy denied non-white people entry into Australia. Both of these illustrate the fact that we separate when we over emphasize differences and ignore the commonality amongst all people and all life on this planet. We can celebrate diversity or we can use it to classify and divide. Hanging on for dear life to our uniqueness, whether straight or gay, makes uniqueness a restrictive quality not a gift.

The gay community is not immune to superiority-conceit. Discussions of who is a 'real lesbian' are based on this. Some lesbians hold the idea that their relationship is automatically superior to that of a heterosexual because it's a woman-woman relationship, and only women can properly love women. This might be the case with some women but certainly not all of them. That's a huge call. I was once told with a great deal of sincerity that if straight women really and truly knew what it was like to love women they would all give up men because lesbian love is naturally superior. There is no equal to it. I have already explained in the previous chapter how this exclusivity argument is not as clear-cut as it appears.

In terms of spirituality and religion, it is also possible to claim some sort of superiority as a result of being gay. Exclusivity, as it applies to religious insight, does not mean having a unique insight due to our experiences as a particular sexuality. There is no doubt that gay people, like any group, transform and shape old practices and doctrines into new and distinct ones. Many famous figures in Buddhism such as Masters Dogen and Nagarjuna found new expressions, insights and methods as a result of who they were and the context in which they practiced. Particular experiences bring new ways of seeing and acting.

Laying claim to a unique insight does not become a problem unless the ego takes exclusive copyright of those insights and markets them as an aggressive and/or exclusive sectarianism. Claiming sole rights to *the* best way is the exact opposite of non-contention or the non-grasping of our own take on life. The next chapter outlines the drawbacks of this in detail. This attitude can be seen in some members of the gay community who claim that by virtue of their sexuality, not only can unique and novel insights be gained, but superior ones as well.

Again, in and of itself, laying claim to the high quality of an insight is not a problem. Some insights are clearer than others. As the Buddha explained however, without panoramic understanding these can be championed as *the* only insights of superior quality. This kind of sectarianism has the potential to become a problem in the *Mahasangha* in the West since it separates people through absolute claims to truth. There is also an aspect of automaticity here. That is, some dharma perspectives may be seen as automatically superior just because they come from gay people. This view promotes the idea that gay people are the only ones capable of true and superior realization.

Zen Master Chinul realized that even though we are innately enlightened, we still need to work on attachments and ego in order to let that true nature shine. All humans face this same challenge. No one is automatically more capable of insight because of their sexuality, color, education or intelligence. People from all walks of life have the potential to be just as capable as each other in the Dharma. Uniqueness does not mean sole potential for quality insight and no one group can own the Dharma. It is for this reason that Kobai Scott Whitney's answer to the question 'Is there a gay Buddhism?' in *Queer Dharma: Voices of Gay Buddhists*, is both yes and no. Yes because we can and do see things in a different light due to our sexuality, and no because the dharma is not just for one sexuality alone. All groups are contained within the dharma. There is no dharma just for us and through us alone.

It comes down to how widely we see. One of my friends once told me that the women at her Mothers Group agreed that their husbands would have a problem if their child was gay. They're loving mothers and caring people, and it is realistic to recognize the discrimination gay people face from not only their family but the wider society as well. My friend assured me that she didn't think it was a problem per se but was worried about the suffering that a gay child might experience. Indeed, if one cares to look, our suffering is legally and institutionally enacted in ways which pop up like red flags. To those who are aware of this, the contrast between gay and straight people can seem stark.

Having heard and seen how my experience differs from hers with regard to the 'biggies' in life (marriage, work and so on), it might seem to my friend that gay people suffer the most. If one group can follow their dreams and another are legally and socially prevented from doing so, the latter does seem to suffer more. And in many ways it's true that I suffer more. However, this is not the only view one can take.

As I said previously, in and of itself there is absolutely nothing unique or special about the suffering of gay people. True, in numerous ways gay people have a more difficult time of it but have you turned on the TV lately? I see heterosexuals robbing, shooting, looting and raping. They start wars in the name of religion and kill millions of people. Through sheer weight of numbers they are killing the planet. Heterosexuals are out of control! Of course, this is a completely selective and narrow view, and one which the media can manipulate. Its bias does not account for all of those times in which heterosexuals do not do the above. As suggested in the previous chapter, without the benefit of a wide perspective we can buy into our views and perceptions as absolute and total reality.

The truth is that if a person is heterosexual, they'll encounter suffering too. There's no mystery why the First Noble Truth was about the fact of suffering — it applies to everyone. Suffering is universal. I'd worry about suffering whatever the sexuality of my child. While straight people have more legal and social ease, they do not miss out on suffering. In fact, there's no automatic guarantee of a better life for any sexuality. I have a wonderful partner, awesome parents, a university education and I work in a job I absolutely love. I have skills and a spiritual path which help me to deal with my own suffering. I have a better and easier life than that of many, many heterosexuals.

Giving up the drug of suffering can be agonizing — our ego loves us to be the one who suffers most. It is painful and difficult to wrestle with *Mara*. In Buddhism *Mara* is sometimes translated as desire itself, or negative desire (for example, the desire to hurt), attachment, neediness, craving or any situation or psychological process where we attempt to hold onto what cannot be truly held. Hanging on to our suffering is to hang on to the special status of 'sufferer.' This is the real problem underlying victim-conceit — the attempt to make concrete what is essentially empty. This impossibility engenders an existential quandary. We try to hang on to what is not permanent in the first place.

Yet it is possible to lessen our pain bit by bit. How we see life and how we deal with it makes the difference between victim-conceit and a more constructive and ego-less recognition of our own suffering. Our teachers and fellow Buddhists can offer us many ways to do this. One way worth considering is acquiring an understanding of the logic of non-contention.

6
The Logic of Non-Contention

In the last two chapters I outlined the benefits of right views — panoramic and non-ego centered. It is also apparent however, that there is a point at which even these views can become unprofitable if we cling to them. This is where the logic of non-contention becomes useful for gay people because in the face of hate and prejudice it is tempting to become extremists ourselves. Non-contention allows us to deal in a balanced way with the questions which arise from feeling separate, afraid, revengeful, hateful, diminished and devalued. It is both an emotional and intellectual approach to our suffering which allows us to bear witness to our pain without adding to it, and without becoming someone who we are ashamed of. It allows us to shift our focus away from uncontrollable outside factors back to ourselves, and in doing so, lessen our suffering.

It must be clear that this is not an approach in which we intentionally play the part of enabler through an attitude of passive acceptance. Non-contention is not passive. It is an active awareness of the world as it is which enables us to prevent our own views from causing contention within our heart-mind. This means we can still work for equality as long as we are not attached to it at all costs. While it eventually becomes ingrained and intuitive, I would like to outline non-contention's intellectual and logical aspects to illustrate its usefulness and utility.

The practice of non-contention is especially useful for us in times when we feel overwhelmed by the pervasive attitudes and views of society, and/or our own strong feelings towards others. The sense of being overwhelmed comes from the fact that position-taking itself is contentious because it involves clinging to one's view and oneself as completely and eternally right. This is in direct opposition to the practice of non-contention, which is that nothing whatsoever should be clung to. In other words, we do not pick one particular viewpoint and cling to it. Gay people need to cultivate this because it gives us breathing space and allows us to approach life with equanimity. This is possible through a moderate mode of living because non-contention is the Middle Way between the unrestrained and restrictive inclinations of life. It is this Middle Way of living that the Buddha advocated.

The Buddha realized that extremes prevent us from reaching nirvana because neither self-indulgence nor self-denial brings peace. In fact, extremes produce mentalities which seek either constant approval or condemnation. This is because instead of seeing all things as relational and interdependent, we judge them by where they lie on a continuum between polar opposites. These opposites are seen as objective realities, the legitimacy of which is taken for granted. We can see this in the schemata we devise to categorize our beliefs. They separate the world into absolutes such as love and hate, virtue and vice, death and life, religion and science, men and women, gay and straight, and praise and condemnation.

We love these dualities, and spend time and money perpetuating the view that they necessarily occupy opposite ends of the spectrum. We think this is automatically the right thing to do because it reflects the total nature of reality. Yet when we believe this wholeheartedly it does not give us the peace we desire. Since we divide the world into concrete opposites, we spend our life fighting against whatever offends us and fighting for whatever pleases us. This view cannot bring peace because it runs contrary to the ultimate oneness of all things. It means that we fight against life rather than work with it, and react rather than respond to life's ups and downs. We fail to see the bigger picture.

As a result, differences and disagreements appear so much bigger than they are because they are seen as representative of a wider reality in which irreconcilable opposites dominate. No wonder we get tired. For this reason, Buddhism considers the Middle Way to be not only avoidance of clinging to opposites, but the direct realization of the essential unity of all things. This non-dual consciousness transcends opposites. It is not limited to daily life categories, concepts and constructs. Neither is it confined to some sort of airy-fairy oneness. This awareness sees both the conventional and the essential, and allows for a panoramic understanding of reality. It can do this because the contemplative mind can hold all opposites at once. It is not interested in analytical and conceptual thinking which separates and compares.

It must be understood however, that the middle path does not mean the mid-point in a straight line between two extremes. Neither is it fence-sitting or an attachment to being neutral because a decision cannot be made. It is a dynamic and reflexive approach which adjusts itself to any circumstance by allowing us to tune our life so that it is neither too tight nor too loose. Zen teacher Charlotte Joko Beck describes it as the middle of a river — deep, free-flowing and fresh. This approach avoids stagnant dualisms by not clinging to either extremes of passivity and action, and enables us to bypass the tendency to polarize into one thing or the other. It also allows us to see that the black and white thinking encapsulated by the 'you are either with us or against us' mentality allows for little flexibility and practicality.

In practical terms, the supreme disincentive to turn away from extremes is seeing how much effort and energy goes into them! I simply don't have the energy to put into full-time (or even part-time) prejudice. The other disincentive is the fact that an angry, hateful person surrenders their life to their emotions. Every time I see a homophobic person begin their rant or I am tempted to go for long-term anger, I am reminded again of how profitable it is not to hand over control to destructive emotions. If we give in to anger, greed and delusion, our very happiness depends on their satiation. This satiation never totally occurs. That is the nature of the world.

Homophobes are perfectly satisfied with their opinions and it may seem on the surface that there is no contention in this at all. In fact, they are absolutely satisfied. Yet herein lies the problem. People who are absolutely and totally convinced of their rightness experience a false calm, and appear centered and supremely confident when espousing their views. Followers of Osama bin Laden reported that he was without doubt. He was assured of the fact that he was completely right in attempting to rid this world of those who didn't think as he did.

He reminds me of a picture I once saw of several Nazi officers standing next to a rabbi. The rabbi had dug his own grave and was holding a scroll of sacred text in his hands. He looked forlorn. It wasn't his face which haunted me the most but those of the officers next to him. They were not gloating or laughing. Their faces reflected the calmness of total rightness. They looked as if they were doing a normal, everyday thing — a thing they were good at and which was justified. There was not one scrap of doubt in their eyes. I cannot describe how ill that picture made me. How intractable and unbending those men were.

Yet underneath this lies a paradox. True and lasting calmness built on contention with the world is impossible because it goes against the very nature of the universe. No one will ever be perfectly satisfied; no one ever totally gets what they want. Recognition of this fact is the only way to be equanimous. This is why the Buddha said, 'I do not contend with the world.' It was not because he did not see the need for change or that he didn't feel he was right, but because he recognized the value of non-contention — the Middle Way. He saw reality.

On a deeper and intuitive level, at some point in our Buddhist practice we realize that it is the nature of the world that we can never cut out those features which we dislike. They may be changed or transformed but nothing is ever lost or deleted. This is because they too are the Dharma. In oneness nothing can be separated out. When we see only the phenomenal and not the essential, we see the waves but not the ocean. We separate objects but miss the essential unity of all things. The Buddha did not miss the forest for the trees. He spoke from a clear understanding of the Dharma.

A surface view sees everything as separate and unequal, but in reality the Dharma or True Law is neither high nor low, bright nor dark, superior nor inferior. It doesn't play favorites and is without preferences. It contains everything and excludes nothing. This is the deeper meaning of only 'seeing one side of things.' In reality we cannot see one side of things because there is no other side. Non-contention is based on this awareness of the nature of the world. Yet bigots place their very happiness on whether or not their needs and wishes about gay people are fulfilled. They wish to cut us out of reality. Devoting time to a cause is one thing, placing your very happiness on the roots of suffering is building a castle on sand.

This is sometimes evident in the approval-dependence which occurs as a result of marginalization. This is when we crave approval from those we know do not like us. This is completely understandable but creates attachment and neediness to the concept of approval. As the Buddha pointed out, if you attach yourself to not wanting to be despised, you're a long way from ending whatever it is that binds you. In fact, you only strengthen it. This is because we place our happiness on outside conditions. If those conditions are not present, neither is our happiness. And so it goes on and on.

Now when I encounter anyone who is intense and extreme, I recognize the external happiness trap. This is a useful thing for gay people to do because it lifts the burden of changing the other person. When I meet someone who is so determined to place their happiness on outside conditions, and who is totally consumed by their anger and negativity, it's almost as if the pressure is off me in a sense. I know that these people are the creators of their own unhappy world and only they can lift the burden. I can only meet them half way. I am perfectly willing to have a civilized discussion, but if a deeply prejudiced person is still determined to bet their peace of mind on gay people becoming invisible and/or cobbled in daily life then that's their problem. I don't even bother contending with this mindset. By oneself one is liberated and by oneself one is enslaved.

This does not mean that we can't hold a view or that to have one is wrong. It does not mean we can't create a political and social system built on views. It does not mean we have to give up our view that we are all equal or that gay people deserve more rights. It simply focuses our attention on the drawback of holding these views rigidly and as absolute truth. It also means that while this insightful recognition helps us to clearly see reality, a still further step is required for non-contention to be truly successful. Right views, while positive in nature, are still opinions and can be clung to.

Truly clear seeing is to be free of any view, however right it may be. It is to see things as they are rather than how we want them to be. The awakened mind sees that everything is interconnected, impermanent and without separate self. From this comes the intuitive understanding that there is no need to attach to intellectual and conceptual understandings. These are important and useful, but in the ultimate scheme of things they are only signs on the highway. When one has seen the big picture clearly, there is no need to make a crutch of constructs and views. As I said previously, we can make use of our conventions without clinging to them.

Needless to say however, ideas are powerful because ideas lead to views which lead to certain kinds of actions. At this point in time there is a struggle between old and new ideas about gay people. These views affect our very freedom because views evaluating whether we are worthy of freedom, may influence how heterosexuals vote. Non-contention does not rule out the importance of views. It does however, draw attention to view-rigidity as the cause of disputes. As the Buddha observed, attachment results in a 'thicket of views' and a 'yoke of views.'

Notice that the Buddha focused on communication which is contentious in nature. In doing this he is not suggesting that we speak only when people agree with us. He simply means that being right is less important in the big scheme of things than equanimity, compassion and contentment. We can see the very opposite of this in the language of some ministers of the religious right, who believe they are doing the best for gay people, but speak in words which convey anything but this.

The 'you've got to be cruel to be kind' angle exemplifies the type of thinking behind conversion therapy techniques and shame-based anti-homosexual programs. The trauma caused by these programs and by religious condemnation is considered secondary to achieving the goal of universal heterosexuality. This illustrates the fact that if we value being right more than compassionate, we have become attached to our own views. It's then that we cause hurt to others and pay for it with the loss of peace of mind. This applies to both straight and gay people.

We can all get caught up in ourselves, especially when we suffer. As I realized with The Spitting Man, I was a bigot about bigots. I had become exactly the same in that my very happiness depended on the absence or presence of a certain thing, namely, him. I had become attached to a certain view. We can all forget that ultimately there is no one to have a view in the first place. We can all forget that acting from what one knows is different to acting from what one clings to. That is, if gay people have discovered for themselves the Paramita of Great Wisdom,[12] which alone sees the fundamental equality of all things, this can inform their action in a profitable way. This is very different from actions which come out of a desperate need for bigots to be who we want them to be, and for life to go as we wish.

In fact, this greed for victim recognition and the need to receive our chosen response is often highly impractical. Our initial response to being attacked is usually to defend ourselves. As anyone who has done this can attest, the most common reaction is what I call the 'Forum Response.' I have found that many people in online forums are simply not interested in other peoples' opinions. They are only interested in imposing their opinion and are not predisposed towards reasoned discussion. If they do ask for another opinion, it is not to clarify an issue; it is to provide an opening for the imposition of their own dogma. In my experience a prejudiced and contentious person is not interested in discussion at all. They want to be right at all costs and a lecture is their preferred mode of communication.

Yet, speaking as an educator, control over others in order to get what we want is often mistakenly perceived in terms of effectiveness. In many ways, controlling a person or a response can seem successful at first. It may feel good to yell at or rant about a bigot. In fact, it can feel wonderful. We can seem to have the upper hand because we've gotten something off our chest. Yet short term expediency does not win out in the end. In the long term it comes around to bite us in the form of stress, anger, bitterness, panic attacks and the nagging guilt that we have become who we yelled at.

This is a very bad feedback loop. Acting with conscious intention and mindfulness helps avoid this. This is especially the case if we

---

[12] Paramita of Great Wisdom — the perfection or cultivation of the virtue of transcendental wisdom.

recognize and work with the logic of non-contention. The sutras contain numerous appeals to the rational and spiritual advantages of non-contention. Even a brief overview shows us that it is no good attacking back if the price we pay for it is to lose control of our emotions and morality. *The Dhammapada* of the *Pali Canon* stresses that if people speak ill of the Buddha or of the teaching (or of anyone or anything for that matter), we should not be overcome with anger or displeasure because this prevents our own self-control. In this state we will not be able to properly assess the intentions behind what is said, and what was accurate or inaccurate. The *Sutta Nipata* states that the wise do not dispute opinions or settle into any view. It asks who we would fight with if we don't set one view against another? There are no 'opponents' if we don't grasp; if we don't dig in for the winter.

This is not limited to Theravadan sacred texts but is found in Mahayana scriptures too. Many sutras stress the relationship between delusion and predatory behaviors. They clarify the link between the greedy need to accumulate things such as position, approval and wealth, and the lack of contentment. This produces anger and resentment, which in turn leads people to prey on others and to think of gaining advantages over them. In other words, ego-centered approaches to life cause contention. The wise understand these links and consequences. These sutras encourage us not to be an unskillful person by understanding how someone becomes a (greed-filled) oppressor. They make clear that an oppressor's greed leads to his own demise. This is certainly not profitable for anyone, and it would destroy the moral credibility of the gay rights movement should we become as driven and as self-righteous as those who wish us harm.

Perhaps the most poignant observation of the disadvantage of contention is contained in the *Flower Ornament Sutra*. It states that if you want to get rid of your enemy, the best way is to realize that your enemy is delusion.[13] In fact, as the *Sutra of the Great Decease* points out, to look outside ourselves for the source of our happiness or unhappiness is impractical and does not recognize the true

---

[13] From *The Buddha Speaks*, edited by Anne Bancroft, ©2000 by Anne Bancroft. Reprinted by arrangement with Shambhala Publications Inc., Boston, MA.

nature of reality or the mind. When we think everything is the fault of someone else, we only add to our suffering. Banking on the bigot to one day recognize us or his own actions is to buy into our suffering and create victim-conceit. Placing control of our happiness in the laps of those who attack us and who are unskillfully hateful is asking for trouble.

When we realize that everything springs only from ourselves, we can learn how to be happier and more peaceful. We can choose how we will react to and perceive any given situation. As the *Guide to the Bodhisattva's Way of Life* recognizes, unruly beings will just keep coming at us. It speaks of them as being as measureless as space. It is impossible to win against them all. If however, we can overcome our own thoughts, this is equivalent to conquering anyone we contend with. We must recognize, the sutra says, that it's impossible for us to control every outside factor. If we restrain our minds, however, then there is no need to restrain everything else.

This recognizes the value of training our minds in the active cultivation of equanimity. The implication of this non-contentious approach is that if we truly recognize the damage done against others through attachment to views, we will not harm ourselves by the same method. Allowing ourselves to buy into our views as total reality is not a practical method of liberation because it is harmful and turns even our bodies into vehicles of contention.

It goes without saying then that non-contention means working with and observing the body. Some practice paths concentrate specifically on the body and the effect of emotions upon the body while others glance at it only in passing. Some paths stress eliminating anger, revenge and hatred totally, while others stress recognizing their ephemeral and causal nature. Whichever the case, every practice at some point recognizes that we cannot know the truth of Buddhism in just an intellectual sense. It must be physical as well.

Discussion in literature about the body in relation to the practice of gay people has so far mainly focused on sexual ethics. For an excellent coverage of this topic please read *Queer Dharma: Voices of Gay Buddhists*. In terms of developing our own Wisdom Path of Right View and Right Intention however, what we do with our bodies in general is an essential factor of the Path. The way in which one uses the body and its senses is very important.

From a Buddhist perspective, human sense organs can be either useful or useless. When we are deluded, we are used *by* our body, but when we are enlightened *we* use our body. While difficult to control and understand, the body is directly linked to the practitioner's development of the perfection of wisdom. It is the instrument human beings have to transmute *samsara* into nirvana. This means that enlightenment cannot happen anywhere else but in our bodies. Our bodies are it.

It is entirely understandable that there are times when we may want to be in any other body than our own. When we experience prejudice there are many times when we are caught in limbo — we don't want to die but we don't want to be in our bodies either. It's just too much to face. What a horrible feeling this is. It can also lead us to use practice as a method of cutting out these feelings. Yet the fact is that our own bodies are intrinsic to a happy life. We have nowhere else to go but here. The Buddha taught that the body is inextricably conjoined with all the activities and sensations of the world. As such, we cannot approach the manifestations of suffering in our lives as just theoretical inquiry. We must recognize and accept them in our body.

This does not mean contending and wrestling with our emotions. It involves recognition and acceptance. Just seeing our emotions changes things and removes any opposition to or guilt we may have in feeling certain emotions. It can enable gay people to have our cake and eat it too because we accept and see our attachments. In doing so, we disempower them through recognition.

Mindfulness of where our fear and anger appear in our body can be scary. It relies on us accepting and mapping out the contours of our stress and anxiety. Basically it means accepting that we are human with human responses. This can be difficult because mindfulness refrains from judgment when we lie at night burning with the fires of anger and fear. Instead, it allows us to work with accepting these feelings. After all, the Buddha did say in the *Mahavagga (Selected Texts)* of the *Pali Canon* that *everything* is burning. That includes our own bodily organs such as the eye, the things we see with it, our thoughts based upon what we see, and the sensations produced by its contact with objects.

This is not just limited to sight but all the other senses as well. That is, the ear is burning, sounds are burning, the nose is burning, odors are burning, the tongue is burning, tastes are burning, the body is burning, objects of contact are burning, the mind is burning and thoughts are burning. The Buddha states that the reason these things are 'burning' is because there is always fuel for this fire — the wood of greed, anger, and ignorance. The traditional Buddhist list of concrete examples accompanies this observation. That is, since everything is interconnected, these three poisonous fuels make *everything* burn with the anxieties of birth, decay, death, grief, lamentation, suffering, dejection, and despair.

Wow. When put in this perspective, our heartburn, bad digestion, anxiety sweats and clenched fists are understandable. We really should give ourselves a break. It is no wonder that in the *Mahavagga* the Buddha also spoke about how weary we become of this:

> Considering this, disciples walking in the
> Noble Path become weary of the eye, weary
> of visible things, weary of the mental impressions
> based on the eye, weary of the contact of the
> eye (with visible things), weary also of the
> sensation produced by the contact of the eye
> (with visible things), be it pleasant, be it painful,
> be it neither pleasant nor painful. They become
> weary of the ear, eye, nose, tongue, body and
> mind. Becoming weary of all that, they divest
> themselves of attachment; by absence of
> attachment they are made free; when they
> are free, they become aware that they are free.

For the first year after coming out I began to have considerable angst about situations or conversations where the topic of homosexuality might enter. In effect, I became a human version of Pavlov's dogs. Ring the bell of homophobia and I would react. In fact, I became super adept at predicting when someone would bring up homosexuality, and this conditioned an anticipatory response which produced intense anxiety. My hearing would become sharp, my heart rate rose and deep in the pit of my stomach I'd feel a sick, lurching feeling.

Many times it felt like the wind had been knocked out of me. I lost complete resilience. Pulled like a puppet, the whole thing was purely reactive. It became so bad that I could not physically bear certain people sitting next to me at lunch time. I couldn't eat my lunch or I'd feel nauseous. It was all I could do to stay seated. It felt for a while that my entire existence was one of contention.

I kept saying to myself, 'This is not how things should be. I shouldn't have to listen to this crap.' I was perfectly right, but by clinging more and more to how things should've been, I ignored how they actually were. I looked outward in an attitude of extreme grasping, and blamed my instability on outside conditions. This was no different to the homophobes I interacted with because their level of contentment directly related to the presence or absence of certain factors too. This is not to say that it's OK for outside factors to be unfair and intolerable, just that the crucial factor for dealing with this is the state of our heart-mind.

Not surprisingly, I often became ill. This is not an uncommon reaction to fear. While we are looking outward for the cause of our illness, inwardly we reflect our distress. Humans have always manifested their problems in their body. We find this in the writings of Buddhism from the beginning. Some sutras talk of the physical manifestations of attachment, such as something blocking the chest, or an internal feeling of living with an enemy.

As I found out first hand, if we do not see the true nature of things clearly, suffering manifests itself when we have to associate with people we don't like and cannot exclusively interact with people we do. Unable to cope, I trod water for about two years. In fact, it is only in the last year that this tendency has decided to only whisper very quietly in the background. It no longer shouts at me. I hear the train coming, I feel the ground shake, hear the whistle blow and the wind whoosh past. Then it goes. I don't know where it goes, all I know is that it does.

This is the result of just watching the body, seeing the transitory nature of all things, enacting some counter measures, watching, and then watching some more. In fact, this is why I love my meditation cushions because they are extremely safe places for the exploration of emotion in the body. No matter how many times we cry or get angry, nothing bad can happen to us if we just sit with it. It is completely safe. At times our ego may make us embarrassed or fearful of what others in the meditation hall may think. Some emotions can also feel overwhelming and we might have to take a break from contemplating them. Yet if we maintain a steadily growing capacity to just observe ourselves, our distress decreases and our pain seems more bearable.

If we take the view that we must feel a certain way then we cannot walk the Path efficiently and compassionately. But if we take the Middle Way, our bodies are not fields of contention. Contention cannot manifest within our body if we are not contending with reality but rather, approaching our lives with non-grasping and observation. Needless to say, manifesting the Dharma in a non-contentious way is one of the most difficult things anyone can work on in their lifetime. For me, meditating and placing faith in the Triple Gem[14] has proven to be the only lasting way to do this. It will be my life's work.

Obviously, non-contention requires a toolkit, and gay people can turn to the Dharma for specific methods to counter greed, anger and delusion. If we examine the Buddha's approach to these roots of suffering we find antidotes which give us a way out. But none of these methods can be effective if they are not grounded on an awareness of the pitfalls of extremism or the advantages of the Middle Way. Once we attune to this, we can effectively walk the Path. This understanding can be enhanced through reading and studying Buddhist writings, especially those which deal with practice frameworks for working with anxiety, fear and hate.

---

[14] Triple Gem — the Buddha, Dharma and Sangha.

7
Reading and Study

When it comes to Dharma study, there are three questions which are important to ask — *what* should we study, *how* should we study, and *should* we study? These questions arise due to the various positions different schools of Buddhism take on the intellectual pursuit of the Dharma as opposed to non-intellectual and intuitive approaches such as meditation and mindfulness. Some Buddhists consider reading and studying as a hindrance to realization, whereas others see it as serving a clarifying or encouraging function. Each of these positions means that different schools will provide different answers to the above.

The answer to the question *what should we study* is limited for gay people in the sense that there are very few books written specifically for us. This is one of the primary reasons I wrote this book. I have done this after the benefit of only a decade of practice. There would be many who would judge this as audacious, ego-centered or perhaps even dangerous. However, for reasons outlined previously, I decided that the benefits outweigh the disadvantages.

Of the few books that do in fact focus on gay people, most centre on sacred text and the experience of men. These are mainly academic in nature and concern sexuality and/or sexual ethics. However, there are a number of useful websites which have information of a very general nature, as well as interesting articles. The following gives an overview of the few books available as well as some of my favorite articles:

> • Brahm, A. (2004). *Homosexuality and other forms of queerness — Excerpt from ajahn brahm.* http://heartlandsg.org
> • Cabezon, J. (1999) *Gay/straight, man/woman, self/other: What would the buddha have had to say about gay liberation?* http://www.enlightennext.org
> • Cabezon, J. (2009). Rethinking buddhism and sex. *Buddhadharma: The Practitioner's Quarterly*, Summer 60-68.

- Corless, R. (2003). *Healing internalized self hatred: Meditations on the lotus sutra.* http://www.gaybuddhist.org
- Dharma, S. (n.d.). *Coming out of the spiritual closet.* http://dharma.fourwhitefeet.com
- Kolvig, E. (2006). *Gay sexuality and the dharma.* http://www. gaybuddhist.org
- Layland, W. (Ed.). (1998). *Queer dharma: Voices of gay buddhists.* USA: Gay Sunshine Press.
- MacPhillamy, D. (1983). *Can gay and lesbian people train in buddhism?* http://www. gaybuddhist.org
- Ritzenheim, M. S. (2006). *Gay buddhists: on a distinctive spiritual path?* http://gayspirituality.typepad.com
- Ritzenheim, M. S. (2008). *How do GLBT folks fit into buddhism?* http://gayspirituality.typepad.com
- Schneider, D. (2000). *Street zen: The life and work of issan dorsey.* USA: Marlowe & Company.
- Shih, Y, (n.d.) *Buddhism and Gay Culture.* http://www. cloudwater.org
- Surya Das, L. (2007). From a spiritual point of view, is homosexuality wrong? In L. Surya Das, *The big questions: A buddhist response to life's most challenging mysteries* (pp. 215-231). USA: Rodale Inc..
- Tollifson, J. (1992). *Bare-bones meditation: Waking up from the story of my life.* USA: Bell Tower.
- Weise, D (ed). (2013). *Perfect light: Personal writings by gay and lesbian Buddhists.* USA: Magnus Books.

The *Buddhadharma* article by Cabezon is the best article about sexual ethics I have ever read. It discusses a modern approach to interpreting the dharma. Search terms related to Buddhism and homosexuality will yield good results from the Internet. Unfortunately, websites with information for those not in the Northern Hemisphere seem to be virtually non-existent in terms of *sangha* listings. Magazines such as *Tricycle: The Buddhist Review, Shambhala Sun* and *Buddhadharma: The Practitioner's Quarterly* can also be searched for material.

By comparison, there are numerous dharma books which deal with the experience of human beings in general. This is not surprising since Buddhism is concerned with the nature of reality for anyone. As such, the assumption that these books are just for heterosexuals because they are written by them is incorrect. Buddhist books, websites and publishing companies now abound, and can be easily accessed. In this sense, we do not lack for material.

I would also like to add that I have found it highly beneficial to read about the experience of other marginalized groups such as African-Americans. While our stories are not the same, there are common threads of experience, and it is enlightening to see how these groups have approached their practice. I can recommend:

> • Williams, A. K. (2002). *Being black: Zen and the art of living with fearlessness and grace.* USA: Penguin.
> • Baldoquin, H. G. (2004). *Dharma, color, and culture: New voices in western buddhism.* USA: Parallax Press.

Being Black is an inspiring and enlightening account of the African-American story and the benefits of Buddhist practice for black people.

It is also illuminating to see how gay Christians deal with prejudice. The Bible does not speak about homosexuality per se because it is a new construct and a new word. Any Bible which specifically uses that word is uninformed. It does however, specifically mention same-sex sexual acts. Due to this it appears that our Christian brothers and sisters are having a much harder time of it religiously than we Buddhists in the West. The following is one of the best books on this topic.

> • Chellew-Hodge, C. (2008). *Bulletproof faith: A spiritual survival guide for gay and lesbian christians.* USA: Jossey-Bass.

In terms of the locating and ordering books, Giovanni's Room, a bookstore with a huge variety of books for gay people, has a very large section devoted purely to gay spirituality and religion, and most of the books mentioned above can be ordered through them. It can be found at http://www.giovannisroom.com. Other online stores also cater to the spiritual interests of gay people:

- The Book Shop (Australia)
http://www.thebookshop.com.au
- Hares and Hyenas (Australia) http://hares-hyenas.com.au
- Calamus Bookstore (USA)
http://www.calamusbooks.com
- Lethe Press (USA) http://www.lethepressbooks.com

The last, Lethe Press, has a collection of books which represent a wide cross-section of spiritual and religious backgrounds. As its website states, Lethe Press is one of the world's leading publishers of gay and lesbian spirituality.

In contrast to the first question, the second, *how should we study* is more easily answered. There is a dearth of material on the Internet about the method and order in which one can study the sutras and Dharma writings. I can recommend *Befriending the Sutta: Tips on Reading the Pali Discourses* by John T. Bullitt on the respected and authoritative *Access to Insight* website. It contains excellent descriptions of how we should approach the reading and study of Buddhist writings.

It is useful to bear in mind that we read for many reasons. It is tempting to view reading in our time-deprived world as primarily for the extraction of information. However, this is not the only way to read. We read for pleasure, for stimulation or for companionship. We read to open our minds and we read to gain direction in our life. In my case, I read Theravadan texts because they are practical, reasonable and rational. They spell out in a logical way the consequences of x, and the method for achieving y.

In some Buddhist sects, just the act of reading or the sacred book itself is considered special. In other traditions, it is studying texts aloud and within a community which is important. Both are emphasized not only because it fosters community and one has access to authoritative voices (the teachers), but also because of the presence of *menju*. This is a Japanese term used to describe the fact that there are some things we cannot obtain just through words, and which can only be learned by sitting face-to-face, hearing a person's voice or having physical contact.

Some texts, due to their very nature, require specific types of reading. In my case, I read Mahayana texts in a different way to Theravadan ones. These texts usually seek to develop insight by debunking intellectual theory through an emphasis upon emptiness. Hearing that there is nothing to debunk in the first place tends to jar one out of one's intellectual paradigms. I do not read these texts if I want intellectual food for thought. In fact, I often don't even understand what I am reading. This sits well with me because this is not necessarily the purpose of reading these sutras. They most certainly do clarify doctrine and hone practice, but not through the intellect. That's because acquisition of wisdom is not acquisition of knowledge.

Catholics have a term for this contemplative kind of reading, *lectio divina*, Latin for divine reading. This is not the process of studying but a meditative way of approaching sacred text. It is not a rational method because it does not involve analysis or the extraction of information, nor does it focus on the accuracy of translation or description. Rather, it is a method which emphasizes meditation and contemplation upon the timeless essence of the text which transcends the words. This way of reading uses the mind which does not seek to obtain anything. In other words, the reader focuses on just being there with the text. They are asked to listen 'with the ear of the heart' until a particular section rises up from the text. A word, phrase or passage may be read over and over, reflected upon and read again. It becomes, in other words, the object of meditation, and is used as a mantra or a means of interior dialogue. Intellectual understanding is not important, but giving yourself to the text and letting the text speak to you is.

While the question of *how we read* is somewhat easy to address, *should we read and study Buddhist writings* is difficult to answer. For some schools of Buddhism the answer is no, for others schools the answer is yes but with qualification. All schools however, recognize that there are aspects or levels of development in Buddhism. Firstly, there is academic scholarship — study and competence in the teachings. This first mode is not the most important but it lets us take one step onto the Path. Secondly, this is followed by putting what one has learnt into practice in order to test out its truth and utility. The aim of this stage is to make the application of the Buddha's teachings a habitual practice. The final and most important mode is the wordless and intuitive realization of the truth.

Nevertheless, early texts talk about how important is it to know a text's meaning and purpose, apply thought to it as we have heard and learnt it, and to fully understand its intent. We should make it so familiar that we remember it instantly. We should also ponder and contemplate the text repeatedly, and fully realize in theory those teachings which the Buddha described as lovely in the beginning, middle and end. Reading and studying sutras are an integral part of the path, but are limited in their ability to foster enlightenment. They get us only so far.

In other words, unless we progress from an intellectual to an intuitive understanding, we will never realize the Way. Not once has a text helped me fully understand a *koan* or point of doctrine. Commentaries have given me direction but have never clinched the deal. In Zen Buddhism, *koans* are brief paradoxical statements or questions. They serve as a point of concentration during meditation and other activities. The effort to solve a *koan* often exhausts the analytic intellect and the will so that an intuitive, non-mediated response can occur. This is designed to instill a profound understanding of Buddhism at a direct, experiential level. Neither my first nor second teacher has ever accepted an intellectual and textual demonstration of my understanding of a *koan*. These sorts of understandings just don't take us far enough down the road.

Doctrine can be far removed at times, and the suggestions in books like this can seem remote. For example, 'no separate self-existence' can be pretty cold comfort when you're sitting in the middle of a group of people who are saying the most dreadful things about gay people — about you. It's natural to think, 'Well if I don't exist as a separate entity, who the hell feels terrible at the moment? It feels pretty real to me!' Even veteran practitioners can fall off the practice bandwagon in times like these and feel distant from the Path.

In the beginning of practice, this gap between words and intuitive awareness can be stark. We read a book on Buddhism and we think we get the idea, but it truly is just that — an idea. In the above example, *anatta* (no separate self-existence) takes on new meaning with time, and the practical implications become apparent with insight. These deeper insights do eventually occur but are not communicable in words, at least not in any way which words can definitively convey. With time, we gradually begin to be panoramic in our understanding. This is not an intellectual thing — it comes from practice. While concepts can help us on our way, gaps between doctrine and experience cannot be reconciled intellectually. Eventually, Buddhist terms and concepts go from being words to a way of being.

While this wisdom cannot be defined, it is however, experienced and demonstratable. This means that gay people can feel free to use reading and studying as a legitimate method of practice provided we see the whole picture. When my intuitive knowledge is not yet developed enough, I know that an intellectual reminder is available. Whenever I think, 'Tell me again why I should do that?' the *Buddha Vacana (Words of the Buddha)* spell it out for me. If I need a reminder of the practical benefits of acting a certain way, I turn to these texts.

There are numerous passages in the *Pali Canon* which outline how to deal with the sorts of situations and feelings which crop up in a gay person's life. That is, the presence of enemies, hate, anger, obsession, victim-mentalities, revenge, restlessness and worry, and stress and anxiety. We can also find descriptions of positive qualities we can develop and the skilful actions which issue from them. On the website *Access to Insight*, these are listed for us and it's simply a matter of clicking on the link to find sacred text and articles on each topic.

At the risk of being accused of Zen bias, I feel it necessary to warn of the dangers of this. It is all well and good to know in theory that reading will only get us so far. In practice, there is the danger of developing a mind which wants an answer from texts. This is simply not possible. At some point, they must be seen for what they are — just signs on the highway. In fact, speaking from personal experience, texts can block more intuitive and deeper ways of seeing reality. If this attachment to 'knowing' occurs, put the books aside and sit. Don't pick them up again until they are just something you want to read, not need to read. There's a crucial difference. At some point, we must put down our belief in the ability of books to enlighten us. Only we can do that.

Due to the possibility of attachment, it is natural that practitioners can encounter warnings against reading and studying. In the Zen school especially, which considers itself as a 'transmission outside the scriptures,' a meditator might find resistance. This is because Westerners often seek to obtain ultimate answers from text. This is an unskillful attitude because essentially there's nothing to obtain and no one to obtain it.

My personal opinion is that we cannot go to extremes. It is possible to be as attached to not reading texts as it is to reading them. Advising people not to read anything is an extreme. Even in the Zen school, many masters knew the sutras well and referred to them in their own teaching. *Koan*s also feature a number of sutras. It seems that well known teachers read and used the sutras in their daily lives. From this we can see that reading and studying are two ways to acquire intellectual understanding, but we must cultivate this understanding in an intuitive sense in order to experience realization.

8
But The Buddha Said So

In the previous chapter I suggested that unless we progress from the intellectual to the intuitive, we will never realize the Way. Text must be made real through an intuitive understanding of reality. This becomes especially important when we consider the role of sacred text in its support (or condemnation) of homosexuality. It goes without saying that Buddhists respect the Triple Gem and consider them authoritative sources. Yet at the same time we must also recognize that while text is a reflection of a teacher's self-actualized knowledge, every teacher, even the Buddha, was a person of their own time. This means that traditional text may not reflect current social customs and attitudes. In weighing up the arguments put forward in Buddhist texts, the tension between these two facts must be acknowledged.

While there are a variety of opinions amongst Buddhists about homosexuality, the current consensus is that the Buddha did not condemn it per se. This is not universally accepted as the case but it is generally perceived as such. His code of ethics for monks and nuns calls for celibacy, regardless of sexuality. Sexual codes of ethics for laypeople are more concerned with sexual misconduct — whether we conduct ourselves sexually in a harmful way. Unlike Christian texts, these do not specifically mention or single out same-sex relations, nor do they issue blanket prohibitions against certain behaviors.

Instead, sexual acts, whether heterosexual or homosexual, are judged by their skillfulness. There are several criteria by which this is judged. Acts are seen as harmful or unskillful if there is no mutual consent, they entail suffering, break existing commitments to another person, lack respect, somehow interfere with attaining enlightenment, and would be hurtful if done to us. In the absence of any specific teachings on sexual orientation and homosexual behavior, it is not unreasonable to assume that homosexuality can be evaluated in much the same way as heterosexuality.

The controversy lies in the fact that some Buddhist texts and traditions prohibit sex without a procreative purpose, as well as the sexual use of certain organs. In effect, this means sex between individuals of the same gender, or with those who have genitals of both genders, is sometimes classed as sexual misconduct. There are also different interpretations as to whether the term *pandaka* (one kind of person unable to enter the monastic *Sangha*), refers to male homosexuals in general, hermaphrodites, or only to those gay men who are 'flamboyant,' exhibitionist or effeminate. For a far more detailed explanation of this I suggest you read the Wikipedia entry for this topic, Peter Harvey's *An Introduction to Buddhist Ethics,* or the Buddhism and homosexuality overview at ReligiousTolerance.org.

In assessing these texts, we must give consideration to the intention and discourse behind them. For example, certain behaviors were sometimes prohibited not because they were ethically wrong, but because they transgressed laws or social norms. The Buddha felt that punitive legal action and social disapproval would make Buddhist practice very difficult, and as a result, he sometimes thought it better not to commit certain acts in the first place.

The implication for gay people is that we have to decide whether to follow tradition or to find our own interpretation and justification. If we do decide the latter, we must accept that we will conflict with prevailing norms and that our authority to do so will be challenged. We may consider ourselves ethically skilful but that doesn't mean other people will, including some teachers. Conversely, societal and religious attitudes can and do eventually change. In the long run, this can result in positive interpretations of texts in our favor.

In fact, it is an error to think that instituting this change will be necessarily impossible or extremely difficult. In the *Sutta Nipata* the Buddha pointed out that designated social divisions in the world have arisen by common consent. He most certainly acknowledged there were divisions in society, but saw them as the creations of man not a divine being. In other words, humans bring ways of acting and thinking into existence, and they can take them out as well. Nothing is written in stone. The impermanent nature of things means that old, outdated modes of thinking and acting have the possibility of being modified or thrown out.

The challenge for those who seek change is the wide-spread belief that teachings are permanent because the Buddha or a respected teacher taught them. This is not restricted to Buddhism. As Candace Chellew-Hodge observes in her book *Bulletproof Faith: A Spiritual Survival Guide for Gay and Lesbian Christians,* many Christians feel that God cannot say anything new. That is, teachings are fixed for all time. Many Buddhists also feel that what the Buddha said was unmediated and definitive. If this were not so, then anyone, even those without the clarity and insight of the Buddha, could claim anything they want.

Others view the teachings as relative to the particular environment and language of their time. While they express universal truths, their mode of expression is affected by context, and this is as true now as it was in the Buddha's time. Supporters of this position cite the Buddhist doctrines of impermanence and interdependent origination. They also point out that a literalist interpretation of tradition can encourage contention because it is based on rigidity and attachment to one way. That way may be inaccessible to large sections of the modern Buddhist community. If the texts cannot speak to us in our world today, then they are dead texts without meaning. The Buddha himself reinterpreted existing traditions in order to make them more accessible and relevant.

It is essential that gay Buddhists also make decisions based on the same sense of compassion, insight and justice that was practiced by the Buddha. This can be difficult given the current ambiguities. These create a double bind for gay Buddhists who wish to respect the teachings but do not agree with all of them. It is hard to belong to a tradition whose text and teachings marginalize you, even though that may not actually be reflected in the daily actions of other Buddhists. It is difficult to balance honoring our Buddhist ancestors and teachers, and respectfully refuting what they advocate.

Unsurprisingly, this divergence means that making a decision about tradition can be difficult. On one hand, it is wise to be cautious about throwing the baby out with the bath water. We can make mistakes and feed our own hubris when we discard anything disagreeable to us. This is sometimes seen in the West in the way in which Asian ritual and folk-religion can be instantly rejected. Many Buddhists in the West have re-oriented Asian Buddhism for a western audience as a return to the 'original' Buddhist teachings and in doing so, cultural differences have been devalued in relation to universal truths discovered by the Buddha.

This is because this filtering process has been greatly shaped by a culture grounded in western rationalism and philosophy. As a result, the Buddha's experience of enlightenment has been equated with the Western ideals of the European Enlightenment. This focus on universals rather than particulars has meant that Buddhists in the West perceive that a pure form of Buddhism exists which can be distilled, so to speak, from its cultural baggage. Some cultural accretions can be superfluous and interfere with the transmission of a message, and their absence makes the Dharma more accessible.

This has allowed for a very pragmatic approach to Buddhism in the West, and has provided for a re-examination of the core of the Buddha's teaching and a consideration of what these teachings mean for people living in the twentieth century. Buddhist literature and publishing houses are also flourishing in the West and Buddhism is on the rise. It is difficult for the lotus to graft to the rock but it seems to be doing very well. This is a direct result of the efforts of many Buddhists, both Eastern and Western, to bring the Dharma to the West, and to orient it to our needs.

On the other hand, this has created concerns over the legitimacy and efficacy of such an orientation. Some Buddhists feel that this has at times resulted in unauthentic, commercialized and untried forms of Buddhism. As well, some of the teachings dismissed as un-Buddhist accretions are actually extremely useful and beneficial despite their unfamiliar and non-Buddhist forms. We must be careful not to forget that traditional and original practices are the foundation out of which our own practice has emerged and as such, should be given due respect even if we choose not to incorporate them in our own practice.

What it comes down to is that gay Buddhists must make a decision about how much credence we give to traditional teachings. In making that decision we are lucky in that we have a religious Disclaimer — we are allowed to question the source of our information and to find the answers ourselves. The Buddha acquired the authority to spread the Dharma because he discovered the truth of the universe for himself. This is the same discovery he asks us to make. In the Zen tradition practitioners are asked to go 'brow to brow' with the ancestors.

In the *Kalama Sutta* of the *Pali Canon* the Buddha asks us not to believe something just because it is in religious text or because a teacher tells us so. This is not a blanket invitation to discard anything a text or person says. He is asking us to weigh everything up reasonably and over time in order to make a sound decision based on our own experiences. Authenticity in Buddhism depends not upon unquestioning belief in the teachings and scriptures, but upon individual and experiential discovery of their eternal truths.

In the *Udana* of the *Pali Canon*, the Buddha talks about how to judge a person. He states that it is only by living with them for a long time that their virtues can be ascertained, and that this requires much thought, wisdom and knowledge. Only by associating for a long time with them in their modes of life can their integrity be seen, and this also requires reflection. This seems a useful suggestion for the way in which we should also judge a text.

It is also apparent that in making assessments of what we integrate or exclude from our practice, we cannot ignore text, and neither can we rely exclusively upon it. I personally favor the Korean Zen approach to the integration of Kyo (Doctrine or Sutra) and Son (Meditation). In the Korean 'sudden enlightenment, gradual cultivation' approach there is room for both, since Son is considered the Mind of the Buddha, and Kyo his speech. Kyo is the mode of academic learning and Son its final intuitive mastery. Unsurprisingly, this approach advocates both scriptural study and the practice of meditation, as long as both are valued and the utility of each is properly recognized.

This is because the Eternal Self[15] is both relative and absolute. The relative pertains to the separate phenomena we see with the naked

---

[15] Eternal Self — the Dharmakaya or ultimate Body of Truth.

eye, while the essential refers to the essential unity we see with our wisdom or Third Eye. This means that doctrines, as well as their textual manifestations, are none other than the Dharma. Yet if we become attached to the words, we miss the essential nature of the world. Conversely, if we think words are irrelevant, we miss the relative. Both are needed for a balance and both are the Dharma. When we avoid residing in one-sided positions this is the Middle Way. Again, as with anything to do with spiritual development, this requires constant self-monitoring.

It is clear that gay people can be in a bind when it comes to choosing which parts of tradition we follow and which parts we don't. We would do well to remind ourselves of the way in which the Buddha asks us to pass judgment. In the *Dhammapada* he observes:

> *A person is not just if they carry a matter*
> *forcefully; no, those who distinguish both*
> *right and wrong, who are learned and lead*
> *others, not by force, but by law*[16] *and equity,*
> *and who are guarded by the law and*
> *intelligent, they are called just.*

We must interpret the Dharma fairly and justly, in accordance with general Buddhist principles, and in ways which do not result in our own social customs and attitudes silencing and marginalizing others.

---

[16] Law — the Dharma.

9
Guilt, Grief and Envy

There is a vast array of emotions that we can feel about our sexuality. Two such emotions for many gay people are guilt and grief — guilt for who we are and grief for who we are not. Another is a sense of envy for what heterosexuals have that we don't. For some of us these feelings last for years but for others they disappear quite soon. Whichever the case, it is sometimes difficult to know what to do with these feelings and where to place them.

To have a sense of guilt is to feel badly about our perceived responsibilities. Just a cursory glance at any thesaurus will reveal that it is considered synonymous with such things as blameworthiness, contrition, disgrace, dishonor, error, failing, fault, and sinfulness. No wonder guilt can become a particularly negative and insidious emotion which can work away at our self-esteem and undermine our faith in our ability to live skilful lives.

Unfulfilled responsibilities for some gay people relate to not living up to the expectations of parents and society. In other words, by just being who we are, we cannot meet the needs of those who require us to be something we are not — heterosexual. Their sense of shame and disappointment can weigh heavily upon us. If we are closeted, we may feel guilty for the fact that those few who do know have to lie to others about us, and that we have given them the added pressure of watching what they say. If we are open about our sexuality, we may feel guilty about the rejection and disapproval our friends and parents suffer due to us.

Such things can place pressure upon family unity and it is not uncommon for some family members to consider the act of coming out as an act of selfishness. For these reasons, a strong sense of guilt can be associated with our sexuality. In light of this, it is useful for gay people to develop ethically skilful ways of approaching guilt that allow us to transform it into something more positive and unfettered.

One approach is to look carefully at the function of guilt. Guilt serves to remind us of the potential for our actions to cause suffering. Although it may seem counter-intuitional to do so, we can come to see it as a positive affirmation of who we are rather than a negative one. In this way we transform the frames of reference we give to our situation. If we place guilt within a negative framework, this perspective serves to emphasize what we are not doing, and who we are hurting. The only thing we can see is that we have caused people pain.

We can also feel stuck — if we cannot change who we are, we cannot reduce the pain of everyone involved. If however, we hold a positive perspective of the function of these emotions we can rework our guilt. By doing so, we can reframe the situation and bring about the possibility of transformation. We can make it less emotional and intense, while still serving a positive function.

The positive function of such things as guilt, regret and shame is to remind us that we do in fact possess the ability to feel these things. If we didn't, we would simply not care that anyone is suffering. It says volumes about us that we recoil from causing others pain. Regret and shame reveal a sense of care and self-reflection. They suggest that we are willing to recognize that our actions have a connection to the emotional state of other people. There are some people who are completely unaware of suffering, or are unwilling to consider ways in which they can be who they are while still employing strategies to reduce the pain of others.

In traditional Buddhist writings we find numerous positive references to guilt and shame. Due to the tendency for guilt to become unproductive and intense, most suggest that it is better to have a sense of shame or regret than guilt. *Hiri,* conscience or moral shame, is a sign of the true contemplative and is the basis for acquiring discernment. It is considered so because those who have a conscience are mindful, and because of this they restrain themselves from actions rooted in ignorance. Without a sense of regret and shame, desire and greed can rule our lives unchecked. As the *Itivuttaka* of the *Pali Canon* reminds us, a person who is shameless is unfit for enlightenment but those who are thoughtful, prudent and reflective can achieve nirvana.

One approach for dealing with guilt is to ask a teacher for particular practices which enable us to constructively deal with and acknowledge any action which may have caused pain. Being gay is not something we are in order to cause pain so we need not feel guilty for that. The inability of others to cope with our sexuality is their problem and not ours because it is their own belief systems which cannot accommodate us. That is their thing and their karma to deal with. So we need not take on any guilt because of who we are.

At the same time, this does not stop us from recognizing that they are suffering, and that our coming out may have triggered all sorts of things which are uncomfortable to encounter. The knowledge that we are gay can cause great distress, negativity and unease in others. In this sense there is some sort of link between our sexuality and suffering, even though there is nothing innately wrong with being gay. We may also have been less than polite or respectful in dealing with their rejection or prejudice. In some cases, we may have acted out of hurt and anger, and said things we later regretted.

If we truly feel that there are things for which we need to atone, and which could have been done in a kinder and more reasonable way, we can approach this in a balanced and appropriate way through rituals, chants, mantras and self-reflective mindful practices. These serve the function of looking guilt in the eye and atoning for any pain we are connected with. For example, in some Zen lineages the ritual of *Sange* is conducted. The *Sange* ceremony is basically a training form for the Precepts,[17] and in many lay practice centers and monastic communities, one evening a month is devoted to *Sange* practice. Some *sangha*s do not conduct group *Sange* but chant *The Verse of Atonement (Sangemon)* at the beginning of each sitting session. In other *sangha*s, members might go further than chanting by considering a precept, and how they met or did not meet this in their daily life.

I chant *The Verse of Atonement* at the beginning of each sitting period at home. I interpret *Sange* as atonement rather than repentance.

---

[17] Precepts — a code of ethics followed by both Theravada and Mahayana Buddhists.

Some people think of it as meaning purification or confession. These are rather forceful words for me so rather than get hung up in distracting interpretations I focus on atonement which carries no negative connotations. Whichever word you use is up to you; it is the intention and sincerity which are important. *The Verse of Atonement* is chanted three times over and consists of the following verse:

> *All the evil karma, ever created by me since*
> *of old; on account of my beginningless greed,*
> *hatred and ignorance; born of my conduct,*
> *speech and thought; I now confess openly*
> *and fully.*[18]

Different schools of Buddhism will have different ways of dealing with atonement and guilt but almost all of them focus upon observation and transformation. In the Tibetan tradition there are a variety of purification practices such as *The Bodhisattva's Confession of Ethical Downfalls*. This focuses on empowerment by emphasizing regret for negative actions, reliance upon the Triple Gem, remedial action, and a vow or promise not to repeat the action.

We need to understand however, that this may not ensure approval (this may never be given), and it may never reduce the suffering and disappointment that others feel about us. But it does bring the possibility of peace and the reduction of suffering ever closer. It can allow us to sleep peacefully at night because we have acknowledged our actions and their effects, and have taken concrete steps to alleviate suffering for both ourselves and others.

In doing this, we must be careful not to take guilt and shame to an extreme. Culpability, another synonym for guilt, can be overcooked. In this way we can destroy the capacity of these emotions to bring about a utilitarian and positive result. Buddhism is not about dwelling on guilt or punishing people for making mistakes. It is about recognizing mistakes and correcting them.

---

[18] From *The Diamond Sangha Daily Zen Sutras*, ©1991 by Robert Aitken. Reprinted by arrangement with the Diamond *Sangha* Zen Buddhist Society, Hawaii, USA.

Once that has been done, guilt, regret and shame are redundant. The *Sutra in Forty Two Sections* states that when a person has:

> personally fulfilled, as far as possible in their
> circumstances, the destruction and relinquishment
> of unskillful actions, understanding the character
> of those actions, avoiding transgression, doing
> what is right, this person, the power of guilt
> destroyed, may obtain reason. [19]

The focus in Buddhism is always upon skilful action and atonement rather than the maintenance of guilt-ridden angst. This is not limited to atonement for just small things either. Even greatly unskillful actions can be dealt with over time.

Excessive guilt however, makes this impossible. The *Dhammapada* points out why:

> They who are ashamed of what they ought
> not to be ashamed of, and are not ashamed of
> what they ought to be ashamed of, such people,
> fall into darkness.

This means that if we feel shame where shame is not due and see error where there is no error, this is wrong view. Delusion and ignorance produce unskillful qualities such as attachment to guilt whereas clear seeing produces skilful qualities such as conscience and balanced concern.

Excessive guilt, the type that wakes us up in the early hours of the morning with a nagging feeling that we are the cause of everything bad or that we are bad through and through, clouds our mind and prevents us from seeing things clearly. This kind of guilt tends to excessively focus on one person — us. This is not a practical or positive thing to do because it is just another type of attachment.

The teachings outline a way for us to moderate these feelings. One overarching approach is *The Eightfold Path* (or Middle Way). This is

---

[19] Reason — offenses naturally dissolve and enlightenment is found.

the path set out by the Buddha to enable us to reach Nirvana. It is the Buddhist Action Plan for liberation. By following it a Buddhist can develop insight into the true nature of phenomena and eradicate the three roots of suffering — greed, hatred, and delusion. The eight elements of the Path consist of Right View, Right Intention, Right Speech, Right Action, Right Livelihood, Right Effort, Right Mindfulness and Right Concentration.

The eight aspects of the path are not taken in a linear sequence. They are interrelated principles which operate in conjunction with each other. It is also worth noting that *right* in this aspect does not mean the opposite of *wrong*. It refers to the sense of something falling perfectly into place and denotes more of a feeling of things as they truly are. By following this path, we can come to feel the rightness of what we do. It allows us to live an ethically and morally sound life. We can also come to see that guilt and shame can be positive catalysts for change. Again, this does not ensure that others morally approve of us, but it does enable us to develop the capacity to deal with this in an ethically appropriate way which minimizes the distress of all involved.

It can also mean that we deepen our insight into the true nature of reality — of what is really going on, and who we really are. This is why observation of our thoughts and feelings is the most basic act of atonement because it allows us to know not only cause and effect, but emptiness as well. As the *Flower Ornament Sutra* states, bad karma is empty in itself. So too are our thoughts and behaviors. If we approach things from this understanding of the essential nature of reality (the type of understanding which arises from sitting with what is), we see that this also means there is no permanent and separate 'me' to be guilty. In other words, there is no final, eternal and substantial stain of shame because it too is empty like everything else.

Of course in a conventional sense there is a you that feels guilt and shame. This is not what this means. It is the wider insight that this you is also, in a very ultimate sense, not an isolated entity but is in fact, everything and everyone. Since everything therefore is one, there can be no two—you and all the rest of the universe. There is just this. Emptiness is what is left over once all the concepts and constructs have been dropped. This is not an intellectual insight but a deep conviction which arises from mindfulness and meditation.

This realization provides the knowledge that everything is guiltless. That is, that Buddha Nature[20] is without suffering, guilt and separateness. Unbridled and overly-reflective guilt can strengthen our attachment to the individual or false sense of self by focusing on how bad we are. It only strengthens the view of the self as an isolated, suffering entity. The recognition of the selflessness of the universe however, frees us from attachment to ourselves and our negative hang-ups about who we are. This egolessness enables us to see that being down on ourselves does not fit with how things are. It denies both the capacity for change and the true nature of things. As with many introspective actions, recognizing this is not the easiest thing to do and takes consistent effort and faith. But it does result in loosening our self-preoccupied grip on the world.

Grief and envy are also other emotions which can affect our mental health. Some gay people envy the surety of acceptance that heterosexuals have, and feel anger at them for not even realizing that they have this. The problem with this is that envy arises out of greed, one of the three roots of delusion. Envy is based on the delusion of comparison, and because of this we want what another person has. It does not matter whether that is an object or a state of affairs. From possessions to acceptance, it is still greed. Needing acceptance is no different to wanting a larger house, great fame or a better body.

Envy is not a stable foundation because it is a perspective of insufficiency. It does not recognize our essential wholeness. This recognition however, should not be used as a disclaimer against fighting for such things as equal rights because ultimately 'there's no one to feel unequal.' In Zen circles this dwelling in emptiness or oneness is called 'Zen sickness.' We still live our individual lives and in many ways we do lack many of the rights heterosexuals have. So there are things we can envy others for if we so choose.

---

[20] Buddha nature — ultimate reality (the true and essential nature of everything) and the interrelatedness of all things.

What I am suggesting is that while envy is understandable, it can paralyze us because its main focus is on what we don't have. As such, it fosters attachment to a missing object or state of being, and it only strengthens neediness and longing. A holistic and centered viewpoint is a non-wounded, and more positive and stable foundation than envy from which to approach what we feel is missing in our lives.

Grief for some gay people occurs because we cannot and do not follow the heterosexual dream of boy meets girl, boy marries girl, and everyone lives happily ever after. Often it is not until we are not the norm that we realize how ingrained our assumptions and concepts are about marriage and what a 'normal life' is. For some of us, this is no big deal. We adapt quickly and realize that we can have perfectly viable and loving families and partnerships which do not match traditional versions. For others, the move from unobtrusive norm to 'gay' causes us to mourn the loss of anonymity. We can mourn for those parts of our world which were less of a hassle and which drew less attention. After going public with our sexuality, some of us grieve for the automatic guarantee that our sexuality will be accepted. We want what we no longer have.

I once saw a documentary about how Western gay people were conducting hand-fasting and marriage ceremonies. At some point, many of the couples had to think hard about how to replace or rearrange traditional terms, costumes and rituals. This is not to say that traditional chapel weddings are unsuitable for gay people, just that the participants were suddenly made aware of how influenced they were by culturally popular concepts. For some of us, losing this dream creates a sense of grief and loss. The loss of the chance to participate in common rites of passage can leave us feeling excluded, rejected and disconnected from society. Even some of our parents go through grief as they realize that the heterosexual life they envisioned for their children will never come to fruition.

It is commonly accepted in the West that grief is a natural and understandable process. Loss almost always engenders feelings of numbness, pining, shock or disbelief, denial, guilt, anger and depression, but also acceptance and hope. Suppressing grief is psychologically harmful. Buddhism is sometimes seen as doing this because it is presented as emotionless, and beyond grief and sorrow. This is simply not true. It would make the Buddha's call to compassion mere intellectualism. Different schools of Buddhism have different ways of dealing with grief, but they all call for looking grief in the eye and dealing with it honestly and compassionately.

Avoiding the issue is not on the list of things to do if we are to approach our lives from a Buddhistic perspective. Loss and envy often leave us feeling that we have a hole in our lives which cannot be filled. A very difficult thing for us to do is put away the fillers, those things we use to numb the pain. This can be food, alcohol, drugs, TV, shopping, gossiping, bullying, and sleeping. We can even misuse practice to numb ourselves or to try to engender blissful states of being. None of these work in the long-term. It is for this reason that all schools of Buddhism suggest there are things we can do which hinder the ability to cope with guilt, grief and envy, and things which can aid us.

As I said earlier, the issue to face for some gay people when we come out is the death of 'normality' and its associated approval. It is indeed as the sutras say — nothing escapes death. A traditional approach to this grief would be to use it as a meditation upon impermanence. Usually this is done upon the death of a person, but in the case of gay people, it can be done in regards to the death of acceptance, 'normality,' and safety. To varying degrees, the old world has gone and a new one has arrived

As the *Sutta Nipata* reminds us, neither young nor old, foolish nor wise escape the trap of death. Everything moves towards an end. My favorite line states that just as all the pots made by all the potters end up being broken, so it is with everything that is created. This may seem depressing but actually it is not. Impermanence carries with it the possibility of change. If things were static we would forever be stuck in our pain. Since things can and will change, there is ever the possibility that we can come to truly understand the nature of whatever we are feeling. In this way we free ourselves from suffering.

For me one of the most wonderful by-products of impermanence has been the loosening of expectations and concepts about who and what people are, and how they should act. My life used to be filled with a lot of 'shoulds.' When I did not live up to my own list of shoulds, I would feel guilty and berate myself for not acting according to certain ideals. Telling my parents that I was gay was the ultimate test for the conceptual walls propping up how things 'should be.' They failed. What a blessing that turned out to be. It opened up a vista of possibilities for different ways of viewing the world.

Since I am gay, I no longer have to carry around many of the expectations which accompany popular (heterosexual) ideas of 'normality' because I can never meet those expectations. What a relief it was to put down that burden. It was frightening when I came out but it was completely freeing at the same time. I never realized how much energy it took to create the picture perfect life. I had bought totally into the big house, nice partner, perfect relationship, kids and picket fence. There is nothing intrinsically problematic with these but attachment to them as absolutely necessary for happiness is. That was the true problem. I never realized how smothered I was in unfulfilled expectations and how trapped I was by my own concepts.

We truly expend so much energy in what we should and might be rather than what we are and what is happening now. I still feel an automatic reaction when anyone disapproves of me but never again will intellectual and emotional constructs get their hooks into my psyche the way they used to. I will never let 'normal' oppress me again. This also means that I am much less judgmental about people, and willing to consider all sorts of ways of doing things. It is good to remind ourselves that impermanence and change can be for the better, and that these can lead to greater insights which benefit us in unforeseen ways.

We can also remind ourselves of what practice is about. In our lifetime we may not ever win approval from some people. But this is not what practice is about. In times when our grief and envy bite deep, it is good to remind ourselves of what our practice focuses on. That is, it does not aim for gain, honor and approval, or the attainment of amazing talents such as the ability not to feel pain. What it aims for is unshakeable freedom of mind. Freedom of mind is to sit on our mats and to feel whatever it is that we are feeling.

With no expectations of feeling otherwise, we can simply feel numb, bitter, sad, angry, envious or self-homophobic. In this way we honor both our experience and impermanence. In this way we do not have to prize off the fingers of guilt, grief and envy, they can fall off by themselves. The separation from our suffering has gone and the ephemeral nature of phenomena recognized.

As a child brought up in the Christian tradition, I loved the part of the Bible where someone persists in asking Jesus how many times we must forgive for it to be right. Jesus just answers simply — if you think it's seven times then do it seventy times seven. Just keep doing it again and again, don't pin it down to just a couple of times and leave it at that. There is deep wisdom in this. I often joked with my first teacher that the default answer for Zen teachers is 'just keep sitting.' They can answer that to every question and it will fit. I fully expect to see a sign on the teacher's mat one day saying 'On vacation: just sit with it.'

Zen Master Dogen knew that just sitting works. There is a wonderful scene in the Japanese movie 'Zen' about the life of Dogen which illustrates his conviction about the power of just sitting. A group of jealous monks from another sect approach Dogen's monastery with the intent to burn it down unless he proves his authority to teach his method of silent illumination. Bring out your proof they demand. Where are your sutras and your statues they shout. Dogen answers that the eyes are horizontal and the nose is vertical. In other words, that reality is right here as it is. That's all the proof we need to live an authentic life. So we just sit and sit until we finally see reality he says. Not getting it, the monks proceed to burn everything down and chase Dogen out of town.

It reminds me of *Koan* Three in the *Book of Equanimity*, a collection of Zen *koan*s. The twenty seventh Zen patriarch once visited a king. The king, expecting that an enlightened person should act a particular way and be accompanied by certain bells and whistles, asks, 'Why don't you recite a sutra?' In other words, an enlightened person should be doing something special. The patriarch replies that he simply breathes in and out, that he does just that and nothing else. He attends to each moment as it is. He is every moment. In this way, he says, he recites millions of sutras. In this story the king illustrates our tendency to expect flashing lights and big guns to remove obstacles. But often simply sitting and breathing can be enough. Simply sitting is enlightenment.

This is one of the best things gay people can do to cope with the demons of envy, sorrow and guilt. If we sit and sit, breathe and breathe, the ineffable transforms these feelings. It is easy to become annoyed at this advice because it can seem like everyone's instant panacea to pain. We Buddhists can pull out these good old chestnuts of wisdom glibly at times. While true, the statement 'there is no you to die' is not really a crowd pleaser either. Sometimes it is positively useless and untimely to say these things. But it still remains that if you are annoyed then sit and be annoyed. It is greatly profitable to be truly annoyed and nothing else. Be so annoyed that the whole world is annoyed with you. It is very difficult to do just this and nothing else. We tend to add in thoughts and worries or create stories out of our fears. But our teachers can give us excellent guidelines for how to do this effectively and for the long-term.

Eventually both the annoyance and how we see it changes for the better. Eventually something happens. We do not need to persevere or to strain with this. The Universe responds one way or the other so there is no need to make it an endurance test. We just have to sit. It was Zen Master Dogen, founder of the Soto Lineage of Buddhism in Japan, who said that no matter how bad a state you may be in, eventually the floating clouds must vanish and the withering wind must cease. Everything changes. In sitting with this it is useful to have faith, a sense of trust that this is what will allow us to heal. It is this trust that I will discuss in the next chapter.

10
Faith

Control is a particularly sensitive issue for gay people as we can often feel that key aspects of our lives are beyond our immediate and daily control. These include laws and policies which restrict us in some way, and prejudicial attitudes which seem entrenched and unmovable. The social and cultural practices which underlie these can seem ingrained in the fabric of society. This is because dominant discourse, the way powerful groups use text to express their attitudes, beliefs and values about marginalized groups, enforces normative control.

These discourses regulate sexuality and defend concepts of what is 'normal' and 'natural.' This is reflected in the very act of coming out. We currently have to announce our sexuality because it is an alternative outside of the dominant way of being, and as such, carries the possibility of sanction and separation. Heterosexuals don't announce their sexuality — they don't have to because it's assumed, is the norm, and carries power and protection.

Coming out is an act of control over our own situation. There are those in our community who forcibly out people who are famous. I understand that the intention of this is to challenge the view that gay people are not successful, and to promote the idea that we are found amongst all walks of life. I hope that those who do this seek a more compassionate way of acting than that which robs people of control over their own life. To take away choice is disempowering and distressing. As a friend of mine often says, 'It's not my choice to tell. It's yours.'

While it is understandable that we are extremely sensitive about controlling as much of our lives as we can, the fact is that there are some things we can control and some we can't. We may want to stop politicians from blocking same-sex marriage legislation in the Senate, but they might do so anyway. Laws may be enacted which outlaw discrimination but it may still happen regardless.

In sitting with this, it can be useful to have faith. Faith gets a bad rap these days. In Buddhism it does not often receive a high profile unless one is talking about the Pure Land School. One reason is because we live in a very secular age, and using faith alone as the basis of proof can seem unscientific and unreliable. It has also been used as the sole justification for some radical religious ideas which are unreasonable and extreme. As a consequence, faith is often associated with uncritical religious belief and rigid dogma. This is not the sense in which faith occurs in Buddhism.

Buddhism makes a distinction between faith as cognitive, and faith as affective. The former is the intellectual knowledge of something without directly experiencing it, or a belief in the existence of something which cannot be proven or disproven. The latter is a positive emotional response to hearing or reading about religious matters, and involves a sense of anticipation and trust. In Buddhism faith is usually regarded as the first step on the path of Liberation. It eventually results in an intuitive and practical knowledge justified by first-hand experience. The Buddhist understanding of faith is almost entirely of this kind.

Faith in Buddhism involves a willingness to test out what the Buddha said by putting intellectual beliefs into practice and judging the results. While faith plays its part, Buddhism does not ask us to believe by faith alone. Our faith must also be a reasoned faith. Uncritical faith is considered impractical, while faith grounded on reason and experience is considered both practical and necessary to enlightenment. Due to this, some Buddhists have suggested faith is not the best word in English to convey the meaning of this practice. Buddhist scholar Masao Abe suggested the term 'boundless openness' might be more appropriate.

If we take the two main Buddhist perspectives on faith we can see why it is of great use to gay people to possess and develop faith. The first is the faith that I can become enlightened, and the second that I am already innately (or originally) enlightened.

Becoming Buddha

This kind of faith can be summed up in five words — I will tread the Path. If I fall down seven times, I will get up eight. In this sense the race is not for the swift but for those who can endure. The traditional version says that discontent does not overcome an enlightened person or suppress him because he endures it. This does not mean we should endure in a weighed down unhealthy sense, but that we should not bow out of the race — we should not give up. Neither does it mean that we are driven in our actions. It means that we continue because we are committed to the Path.

This kind of faith involves acting on the belief that it is possible to find peace, and with an intention to discover what the Buddha discovered. Traditionally this has been the faith attitude of Theravada Buddhism. It is the recognition of the fact that the Buddha was a human being, and as such, we too can do what he did. We hear what other Buddhists have to say and see if what they are saying is true for us too. While we cannot control some things, we can control our own attitude to practice, and we can act on that attitude.

Testing out the Buddhist Path is perfect for those who lack trust and are suspicious of dogma and authority. It is perfect for those who have been told to believe they are either inherently evil, have chosen a dysfunctional 'lifestyle,' or that they engage in abominable acts of sexual deviance. The authority with which some people, particularly religious figures, make pronouncements upon our nature, can sometimes seem overwhelming. Blind acceptance of this authority has had dreadful consequences for gay people.

Until recently, for example, the myth of the gay person as sexual predator has been the authoritative version of homosexual behavior. Some time ago I was privy to a discussion about student protection between several beginning teachers and an older teacher. A primary school in the area had just reported a strange man in the toilets. The veteran told his audience with absolute authority that we must be 'especially vigilant' about these homosexuals because it is young people they target. He painted a picture of hoards of homosexuals lingering near schools in order to abuse or 'convert' young men and women.

My all time favorite and incredulous take on gay people is contained in *The Pink Swastika*. In this book it is stated that gay men in Hitler's inner circle played a central role in the Holocaust and Nazism. The persecution of homosexuals in Nazi Germany, the authors maintain, is the myth of the 'pink triangle.' This book has been used extensively as an authoritative text by anti-gay crusaders. If we look at the reviews on Amazon.com we can see that many reviewers regard it as a serious, scholarly work. It has even been used to draw attention to a supposed link between Satanism and homosexuality.

I once taught next to an instructor who conducted health classes for teenagers. When my class was quiet I could clearly hear his lessons. Many times I heard him teaching that gay people were the highest risk group for AIDS. The truth is that, as a gay person, I am in one of the *least* risk groups. He never mentioned gay people of my gender. Also, while this disease was most prevalent among gay men in the 1980s, the spread of AIDS among this group has slowed in the last two decades. The rate of AIDS in other groups however, such as heterosexuals and intravenous drug users, continues to rise.

In the last ten years, heterosexually acquired HIV has become the largest category of newly acquired AIDS. The AIDS picture is far more complex than the one he taught and tested his students on. Passing his tests required mastering misinformation and acquiring an over-simplified picture of reality. It is important that people in positions of authority do not institutionalize incorrect facts or stereotypes, not to mention that proper instruction necessitates up-to-date information.

Sometimes we cannot help but believe what people say about us. We are all products of our upbringing, and if we have been brought up in traditional religious families or authoritarian families, it is difficult not to obey this authority. It is difficult not to believe that there isn't something wrong with us. Yet the Buddha asks all of us to see for ourselves what the real deal is. In doing so, many Buddhists have taken on board the Buddha's famous answer to the Kalama people on what to believe and trust. He cites ten specific sources which are not to be accepted as automatically authoritative without further verification. These are revelation, tradition, general information sources such as gossip, sacred text, logic, philosophy, common sense, private opinions, experts and our own teachers.

> *The Kalamas of Kesaputta came to the Buddha*
> *and said: 'There are some monks and teachers*
> *who come to Kesaputta. They talk a lot about their*
> *own ideas but they despise and take to pieces the*
> *views of others. And as we listen to them, we can't*
> *help feeling some doubt. We waver between who*
> *is telling the truth and who is telling lies.'*
>
> *'It's a good thing that you do have doubt, Kalamas.*
> *You may well waver, for your wavering is all to do*
> *with a matter that is wide open to doubt.*
>
> *So listen to me, Kalamas. Don't go by gossip and*
> *rumor, nor by what's told you by others, nor by*
> *what you hear said, nor even by the authority of*
> *your traditional teachings. Don't go by reasoning,*
> *nor by inferring one thing from another, nor by*
> *argument about methods, nor from liking an*
> *opinion, nor from awe of the teacher and thinking*
> *he must be deferred to.*
>
> *Instead, Kalamas, when you know from within*
> *yourselves that certain teachings are not good,*
> *that when put into practice they lead to loss and*
> *suffering, you must then trust yourselves and*
> *reject them.'*[21]

This is not limited to heterosexuals. The Buddha is also asking gay people to work out for ourselves who to trust. In effect, he hands the control to us. In this way, no matter what people believe or what we hear and read about ourselves, *we* decide what is true and what is not. *We* are in charge of our heart-mind. Here is the committed faith that we can become bodhisattvas whatever the conditions and no matter how much we doubt our self worth.

---

[21] From *The Buddha Speaks*, edited by Anne Bancroft, ©2000 by Anne Bancroft. Reprinted by arrangement with Shambhala Publications Inc., Boston, MA.

One of my favorite novels is Anne Rice's *Interview with a Vampire*. In this book the vampire's brother receives a vision from God, but no one can believe he is so knowledgeable because he is just a brother, a son and an ordinary person. Eventually the brother commits suicide because all of his family thinks his vision of a better world is pure vanity. Surely just an ordinary person cannot know things reserved for prophets. A prophet is a special person with special knowledge. An ordinary person cannot realize the truth as well as a special person.

This is precisely how gay people should not think if we are to live well. We must have faith that ordinary people, even less-than-ordinary people, can be Bodhisattvas. Bodhisattvas are the ordinary people we see around us who have made the Path their everyday life. In fact, they are us. No one needs to be special to have Buddha nature. In this sense developing the faith that we can become Buddha is to learn to see that we all have skills and capabilities. Acting from that knowledge is the way to be true to our daily life.

As Master Linji, founder of the Rinzai Zen sect once pointed out, we must have faith in ourselves rather than rely on outside things. He suggested that if we look everything squarely in the eye with a sense of trust and faith, reality becomes apparent of itself. For this reason, he advised:

> *Just put your heart at rest and seek nothing*
> *outside. When things come towards you, look*
> *at them clearly. Have faith in the one who is*
> *functioning at this moment, and all things of*
> *themselves become empty.*[22]

Just trust what is functional in you — what great advice. Gay people are often portrayed as dysfunctional, the result of a dysfunctional upbringing (i.e. an overbearing mother or father) or as the creators of dysfunctional families if we have children. Yet Master Linji says that there is something functional in all of us

---

[22] From *The Zen Teachings of Rinzai*, ©1975 by Irmgard Scholegl. Reprinted by arrangement with The Buddhist Society, London. http://www.thebuddhistsociety.org/

without exception. What is it that is functional? Our Buddha nature, the ground of being. Faith as an expression of being Buddha concentrates squarely on this.

Being Buddha

This kind of faith can be summed up in one word — this! It is the intuitive appreciation of one's own inherent worth which is also this world's inherent worth. This involves cultivating an attitude which does not aim to achieve enlightenment, but to continually reaffirm what we already are — Buddha. It is the process by which we continually deepen our insight into our original nature. Traditionally this has been the faith attitude of Mahayana Buddhism. This is an important attitude for gay Buddhists to take for two reasons — it allows us to see Buddha nature in all people and things, and in doing so, to conjoin ourselves and others. It lessens and/or erases the gap.

When we aspire to deepen our insight into our original nature, this eventually involves the recognition that others are actually us. In the *Song of Zazen* Zen Master Hakuin states unequivocally that by their very nature all beings are Buddha. No one is without the capacity for Buddhahood. This also means that there is no Buddha nature for gay people and another for straight people. It is all One. This poses two difficulties for gay people. Firstly, many of us suffer from self-homophobia and feel very separate to others, and secondly, that it is incredibly difficult to consider our antagonists as ourselves. Perhaps we even reject the utility of doing this.

Acknowledging our original nature means giving everyone a break, including ourselves. It might be that we think we have to be perfect before we begin practice or before we realize anything through practice. This is not the case. In fact, this kind of faith negates these notions. It focuses squarely on the fact that for centuries Buddhists have been talking about everyone's innate nature, and that at any time a practitioner can seek to find out for themselves the truth or falsity of this. Herein lies the difficulty for those gay Buddhists who experience self-loathing and self-homophobia.

Self-homophobia manifests in a number of ways. We might have hurtful thoughts and feelings towards gay people, or be in extreme anger or denial about our sexuality. This results in a lack of self-acceptance, and sometimes in depression or suicidal thoughts. There are many things which tell us that we are strange, deviant or different. Not surprisingly, the suicide rate for gay people is disproportionately high to the percentage of population. Substance abuse, violence and anxiety in the gay community are the direct result of societal rejection and disapproval.

Even in cases where self-acceptance is high and a supportive family/friendship group exists, self-homophobia can present from time to time. In my case, it rarely occurs now, but if it is to occur, it will be at a time when there are repeated incidents within a short time frame. These usually involve people talking about homosexuality using extreme and negative words. Often I am not aware of how this has tainted my feelings until I get home and feel like something is crawling under my skin. Self-acceptance, let alone acceptance of the fact that we are Buddha nature itself, can be an uphill battle. However, it is impossible to be at ease with others unless we are at ease with ourselves. Faith in our innate worth is one way to find this.

Having faith in our own Buddha nature also requires faith that that same quality exists in others. This necessitates accepting that the former cannot exist without the latter. When we are subject to hurtful words from both ourselves and others, it builds walls which militate against this. When we are being victimized and are angry, who the heck wants to see the value in our attacker! Often it is completely confusing to have people whom you love and respect hate you. Parents who reject their gay children outright are good examples of these. How do you even put this together in your head? In fact, the reaction of many of us to seeing others as ourselves is strongly antithetical. It can seem crazy and unrealistic to some gay people to even be in the same room as homophobes.

In the early years of his ministry, Malcolm X, an African-American Muslim minister and advocate for the rights of African Americans, was asked why he wanted to live separately from white people. He strongly responded by saying that he did not wish to integrate with a people destined to decline and who were synonymous with the devil. Needless to say, the Hajj pilgrimage to Mecca revised his views and he indicated new perspectives after that. It is indicative however, of how we feel when others suggest we should even be on talking terms with those we identify as threats and oppressors.

To ask gay people to have faith in the equal and identical nature of both ourselves and those who hurt us can seem like a request to live in la-la land. It can seem like unrealistic, wishy-washy Gandhi stuff. Yet the truth is that when we develop faith in our own original nature, we are also developing faith in the power of mutuality because the real nature of reality is all-inclusive. This recognition allows us to be at peace with others because we can see the whole picture and not just a partial one. A partial view affirms partiality whereas a total view affirms equanimity. We realize that those who seem so different to us are only so on one level. On another level it's simply not true that there are any differences at all.

Faith in the truth of this fact is liberating. Faith in our innate nature also allows us to entrust everything to Universal Mind. Universal Mind is simply another way of speaking about Buddha nature. There are many ways of expressing the fundamental principle of ultimate reality, each emphasizing different aspects of the same thing. To speak of *Buddha Nature,* for example, allows us to speak of realizing the whole by recognizing that we as individuals are the Universe, and as such, each of us can become a Buddha. *Universal Mind* (or original mind) lets us realize that all individual things are the whole. This angle on ultimate reality focuses not on the individual as a reflection of the whole but the whole itself — the unified consciousness and undifferentiated ground of being.

So these interchangeable terms are just different lenses for looking at the same thing. I take great encouragement from sitting with a sense of trust that Universal Mind can solve everything. This is one method of affirming our Buddhahood because there is no difference between Universal Mind and ourselves. To entrust everything is to have faith that we are the Eternal Self, the ground of being. This does not mean having faith in Universal Mind as if it were something outside of us or an object within us because everything, including us, is Universal Mind. It's just faith itself as an expression of Universal Mind. It is an expression of Universal Mind because there is nothing that is not Universal Mind.

All things are intimately connected. This state is the world of perfect unity where there is no separation between faith and Mind or us and Mind. Meditational awareness is therefore synonymous with the act of authenticating or empirically verifying Buddha nature. It *is* Buddha nature. Faith leads to practice, which is both one with and a means to enlightenment. The *Ten Verse Kannon Sutra* states that this moment springs from (Universal) Mind and this moment itself is (Universal) Mind.

This is the same realization of the Buddhas and patriarchs, of one's own identity with everything else. In essence, it is the realization of non-duality. This means that we don't practice to become perfect; it is an expression of our perfection, of who and what we already are. Since it is not based on a subject-object perception, that is, *I* have faith *in* something outside of me, this kind of faith does not require an object and is not limited to specific people and things. It simply is. We are entrustment. This in itself is an affirmation.

In this view, enlightenment is not a one-off realization experience, but a continually mindful state and a way of life. It is for this reason that faith leads to a radical transformation of consciousness — the affirmation of one's own Buddhahood. As the *Flower Ornament Sutra* states, those who realize that their minds are not fundamentally different from the Buddha's are already Buddhas.

This means that we do not need to intellectualize anything or turn to another source for our happiness. Steadfastness can be achieved without needing theories, sutras, words, chants or advice from others. In other words, we let Universal Mind do its work. Eventually the clouds must vanish and the winds cease.

This kind of practice can be healing for gay people who feel they have little control over their lives and their own identity. To continually entrust and let go is frightening but liberating. Bit by bit we can maintain the affirmation of our Buddha nature. In doing so, our faith and our knowledge of the inseparability of ourselves and others are strengthened. To entrust regularly lightens our burdens because we need do nothing but entrust — to literally *be* faith as an expression of who we are.

In some Buddhist traditions, faith by itself brings salvation. Most commonly however, faith and practice together are considered the raft by which one crosses to the other shore. They work in unison. Zen Master Kao-feng Yuan-miao of the late Sung Dynasty advocated faith accompanied by the act of looking into 'the tiger's den.' With this phrase he is suggesting that we discover our Buddha nature not from outside things but from our faith in who and what we are. This knowledge is the natural product of faith, but it must be a complete faith enacted in life for any realization to emerge. He is suggesting that faith must be accompanied by practice, that we must be brave and look into ourselves to do this. Freedom is found right in the thick of things.

In terms of practice, 'looking into the tiger's den' is usually manifested in two main ways — bailing out our boat and letting ourselves float. Both of these are extremely useful to gay people.

11
Bailing Out the Boat

When it comes to practice, the choice of which path to take can seem bewildering. Traditionally, practitioners have been offered two main approaches. The first, which I have coined 'bailing out the boat' is the practice by which I can become Buddha, whereas the second, 'letting yourself float' is the practice which develops the realization that I am already Buddha. The former has been the approach favored by Theravada Buddhism and some Mahayana schools such as Soto Zen, whereas the recognition of Buddha nature is used solely by Mahayana Buddhism.

Methods differ from tradition to tradition, and I will not attempt to outline them here. However, I would like to explain, from the perspective of what is useful to gay people, why these two approaches offer important practice aspects to consider. Sectarians might say that one path is better than the other, but in actuality, both paths are equally viable for gay people. Many practitioners use a combination of both approaches since it is beneficial and skilful to look at our phenomenal, transitory delusions, as well as our essential wholeness. For this reason, I would also like to focus on the concrete results of these particular practice attitudes.

The first method, bailing out the boat, is based on continuous effort and founded on intention. The benefit of this approach is that intention can develop depth over time. Once my friend and I were talking and I said that I'd like to get to the point where I wouldn't hesitate to help a bigot if he was in trouble. She said with a shake of her head, 'But that will take years.' While this is true, better that be my intention and my life work than not. I'd rather live continually with that vow than be mired in suffering and hate because intention is very important for liberation. In fact, so important is intention to liberation that it is listed as one of the essential aspects of the Eightfold Path.

Together Right View and Right Intention are the parts of the path that cultivate wisdom. This wisdom can develop and deepen if our intention to bail out the boat remains steady. Our thoughts and intentions are important because they condition our actions and therefore, our karma. When we understand this, wisdom is gained. The Buddha drew specific attention to this relationship in the *Dhammapada*:

> *All that we are is the result of what we have*
> *thought: it is founded on our thoughts, it is*
> *made up of our thoughts. If a person speaks*
> *or acts with an evil thought, pain follows them,*
> *as the wheel follows the foot of the ox that*
> *draws the carriage.*
>
> *All that we are is the result of what we have*
> *thought: it is founded on our thoughts, it is*
> *made up of our thoughts. If a person speaks*
> *or acts with a pure thought, happiness follows*
> *them, like a shadow that never leaves them.*

Clearly, what we think and feel is as important as what we do. It is important to remember however, that since Buddhism considers emotion and intellect to be virtually inseparable, the result of our thoughts does not mean the intellect per se, but what comes from the heart-mind. In fact, in some Asian languages the word for heart and mind is exactly the same. It is also useful to note that few translators now use the words evil and pure. More common is the use of words harmful and harmless in recognition of the fact that Buddhism focuses more on the skillfulness/unskillfulness of actions rather than a good/evil dichotomy.

When I came out but could not tell people at my work, I became confused about whether I was deceiving my peers and students by not being openly gay. My teacher's reaction was to focus on my intention. She asked whether my intent was to deceive, or to teach well and help my students. Since the answer was the latter, it was obvious she had purposefully drawn attention to the link between intention, action and karma. While it still does not sit entirely well with me, I now focus even more intently on developing Right Intention within the context of Right Livelihood.

Right Intention counters wrong intention and is the antidote to unskillful karma. Bit by bit it allows us to lighten the burdens caused by wrong views which emphasize the self and reinforce the ego. The Buddha drew attention to the efficacy of this approach in the *Dhammapada* when he stated the following:

> *Empty this boat!*
> *If emptied it will go quickly;*
> *Having cut passion and hatred.*

If the boat looks like it's going under, we know we can bail out enough water to keep going. If we are stuck in a groove, we can also untie the rope which keeps the ship fixed and motionless. This is why the word passion is used in some texts, since it implies a knee jerk reaction in response to strong emotion. When we have this, we are not bailing out the boat, we're putting more water in. We're attached to the boat. We do destructive things and don't want to move to the other shore.

When we truly see what is happening, we can employ strategies to lighten the load. It might be that we can plug a few holes or even repair parts of the boat. The traditional interpretation is that we find release when we see that all things are impermanent, interconnected and that there is no separate self. This in turn releases our tight grip on the world and we learn not to own our suffering. Instead of it being our suffering, it is just suffering. We learn to just be. Eventually we can reach the other shore. Things become lighter when we take steps to deal with them.

This necessitates that practitioners cultivate a conscious intent to train their heart-minds in a certain way. This transforms the need for control and power into an intentional positive action plan based on Right Understanding. This is where gay people have great opportunity in their daily lives to bail out our boat. As homophobia thrives in certain sections of our society, there is ample opportunity to work on ourselves and much grist for the mill.

As I said previously, the words used to express and enforce dominant discourses reveal much about society's underlying attitudes to gay people. Over the last ten years I've heard that we should be shot, castrated, hung, bashed or jailed. This has come from not only those easily identifiable as intense homophobes, but also seemingly reasonable and open-minded people. Often the implications of this and the hurt this causes are not fully seen because the object of this is a 'gay' — a mysterious 'other.' Labels de-personalize people and create distance so that the real and personal implications of our language are removed. This is one reason why the suffering of gay people can sometimes be completely unseen.

In educational settings, for example, just calling someone gay is a powerful weapon. It's an effective method of censure for teenagers. I often encounter the ubiquitous 'That's so gay.' This is not an expression usually used outside of Teenage World but it is a powerful and revealing phrase nonetheless. It shows us many things about inherent attitudes towards both gay people and anyone or anything outside the circle of approval. It clearly reveals who has control through the power of disapproval.

In my classes I ask my students to find another way to express dislike because those particular words can make some people in the class feel unsafe. The usual defenses are: 1) we mean nothing by it, 2) everyone says it, and 3) we don't actually mean 'homosexual,' we mean 'bad.'

It's certainly true that students often mean nothing homophobic by what they say but there is an effect nonetheless. Gay teenagers experience much bullying at high school and many of them recount experiences of feeling singled out by the language other students use. A gay student can hear 'That's so gay' as many as 10 times a week. This amounts to thousands of occurrences over a five year period. There is no way that this does not have some effect. Despite occupying a low percentage of the population, the disproportionately high numbers of gay youth suicides indicate that a significant proportion of gay kids feel insecure and threatened. If there is even a remote chance of *anyone* in my class feeling threatened, I would rather use alternative ways of expressing opinions.

Having said that however, things are not so clear cut. Even some gay students themselves use that phrase. We are all products of our environment in one way or another and words are used for different purposes, not all of them prejudicial. Yet the phrase does represent the complete hijacking of a word. The majority has taken control of what has been purposely chosen by gay people as a positive descriptor, and turned it into something to describe anything negative in the world. Now anything which is frowned upon is connected with the word gay. The scope of what the word 'gay' covers has taken a giant leap. There is no way that this does not reflect or reinforce in some fashion the power structure of society. It is difficult to imagine 'That's so straight' ever being used with the same dominance, power, frequency and ubiquity.

Every time I think of this phenomenon, the title of Alice Walker's article about the insidious effects of prejudice, *Suffering Too Insignificant to See*, comes to mind. Yet these things add up to form a bigger picture. Unless we isolate ourselves totally from the world, we can't stop societal attitudes about our sexuality from coming into our living room. Advertising agencies will tell you that it is the golden rule not to feature just two men in ads because they will be perceived as gay, and gayness puts people off buying the product. If there are two men they will almost always act in a way which makes it clear that they are straight, especially if there's some form of physical contact displayed.

These types of reactions are typical of the accepted and frequent ways in which straight people role-model attitudes to anything perceived as gay. They are demonstrated often but fall almost completely under the attention level of the general public. To many heterosexuals the above example may seem like a little thing, because by themselves, small things are often just that — small. For this reason, we are sometimes asked by heterosexuals why we can't take a joke, and why we take offense to particular comments when people 'don't mean anything by it.' One Australian editorial recently argued that the Generation X use of the word faggot doesn't reflect homophobia; it's just a common expression to indicate a lack of coolness.

But nothing exists independent of culture and discourse. While the phrase 'That's so gay' may often not be directed at gay people, it would be unrealistic to consider it the only phrase in the English language disconnected from other contexts. For this reason it is over simplistic to say that it has no effect and over simplistic to say that it is always prejudicial. The word black, for example, can just mean a color, but it cannot ever be severed from its other referents. Different meanings, both innocuous and prejudicial, may apply depending on context and intent. So too then the phrase 'That's so gay' is never completely isolated from its homophobic connections. For this reason, Right Speech and exercising self-control and sensitivity is important in a classroom context.

This is important at this point in time because a balanced way of speaking about and representing us does not presently exist. If what we see of a subject or a word is almost always connected with some sort of negativity, negativity is what we get. Even if 'not cool' isn't in reference to sexuality, that provides little comfort when you're being beaten up over it. Even if you aren't actually a 'faggot,' it's hard to have a sense of humor when you end up in hospital because you've been identified as one.

Like small and ubiquitous negative comments, that's not a little thing. It is not a joke if you are on the receiving end of this because there are daily repercussions of such role-modeling in our lives. Nevertheless, the editorial was quite right in suggesting we need to loosen up. When we lose our sense of humor we become grim. Rather than shrug off any negativity with an indifferent laugh, we can use what comes our way to lighten our burdens. Obviously, there is much grist for the mill in our daily lives.

This is why bailing out the boat is an especially useful approach for us. We have been handed our deliverance on a platter through frequent and intense opportunities to work with our own ego. We are fortunate in this sense because the impetus to practice is always before us. This is of benefit not only to us, but other marginalized groups as well. The need to inform and educate is crucial for any group or society who wants equal rights. A large part of the African-American struggle for equality has involved lifting the level of awareness about what it means to be black, and to reflect on the ways in which language and the media are used to convey that. When people really see the link between words, attitudes and power, a transformation can occur in terms of taking personal responsibility for the ways in which our language maintains prejudice in the daily lives of others.

I truly feel that many of the negative ways in which gay people are talked about are not consciously orchestrated. Many straight people are simply ignorant when they speak about gay people, just as one group can be about other groups, and just as anyone can be about anything of which they have little knowledge. The Buddha took this attitude too. He called unskillful people fools rather than evil because it is ignorance not evil which is the primary cause of suffering. In his case however, he meant ignorance of the true nature of reality — that people did not really see.

After coming out I looked at the term 'gay' in a new way. Obviously it now meant something personal to me. For the very first time it entered my mind that conversations about gay people were in fact about *me*. It was no longer about some unknown person I didn't care about. I began to think what it actually meant to call someone a pedophile when they weren't. I began to see how we perceive all sorts of groups in society and how we stereotype and separate. It was a real eye-opener.

To my dismay I also found that some gay people used ideas and language against other groups, and even other gay people. Despite knowing how it felt to be on the receiving end of such things, they still did it. In fact, I sometimes did too! What a blow to my image of myself as a fair and even-minded person. It's ironic that some of us say the same sorts of things about other groups (such as refugees) that are said about us — they carry diseases, they won't fit in and so on. It is a measure of the negative influence of greed, anger and delusion that our choice of weapons against other groups can be the same ones used against us.

Dealing consistently and compassionately with our own ego and prejudice is better not only for our own group, but the whole of society as well. The way in which we perceive the world is a direct reflection of what is within us. In other words, our frames of reference are the filters through which we perceive everything. Our self-knowledge and sense of equanimity can help and encourage others when they suffer, or our sense of ego can make things even worse. How we interact with ourselves is important to how we interact with others. If we can bail out our boat enough to sail smoothly, that's when we can take other things and other people on board.

The concrete result of bailing out the boat is that suffering can eventually take on different dimensions. Martin Luther King once said that we must believe that unearned suffering is redemptive. I know this is as totally true for me as it is for any other gay person. It is redemptive because when we take a constructive attitude towards suffering it has the power to transform us. This occurs because we see suffering as an opportunity to train our heart-minds. We train ourselves to consider suffering as the key to getting our act together. When we do not have this attitude, everything is a potential source of unhappiness. It can be really beneficial for us if we take a Buddhist perspective and see problems not as 'problems' but as teachers.

In order to do this we need to do what might seem counter-intuitive. It is instinctive to run away from pain. Even small insects do it. There can be a lot of pain in the lives of gay people and it is natural that we want to get as far away from it as possible. But if we don't run from the pain, and instead see it as necessary to our development, then things improve. This does not mean forcing ourselves to remain in a situation where we are subject to sexual, physical or emotional abuse because our practice involves facing suffering. Pain for pain's sake is not what this is about. It does not entail placing ourselves in harm's way.

Facing pain as it is meant here is primarily an attitude, and involves gradually training the heart-mind to see and use suffering in a particular way. It may not seem like it in the beginning but ultimately it is an act of kindness to ourselves. If we understand the difference between a necessary and sufficient cause, we can understand why this is so.

A sufficient cause is something which is enough but not necessary for another thing to happen. If I am tired, for example, I go to sleep. Being tired is enough or sufficient to make me sleep. Yet there are other causes which create the same result. I can go to sleep when I'm not tired because maybe I know I have to get up early and I don't want to miss out on sleep time. So being tired is certainly one reason which can make me go to sleep but is it not necessary for me to be tired to sleep. Perceived as a sufficient condition, the presence of suffering is one way to engender enlightenment, but it can happen without suffering and by other means. If we see suffering as the necessary cause however, it is the condition upon which enlightenment occurs. That is, for enlightenment to occur, suffering must be present.

This is evident in traditional Buddhist cosmology, where the most beneficial realm to be born in is the human one because of the existence of suffering and the presence of Buddhist teachings. It is suffering which spurs us on. The God realm does not contain suffering but only pleasure, and so is not beneficial at all for practice because there is no motivation for enlightenment. It was no coincidence that The First Noble Truth and not the Third focused on suffering.

Right from the beginning of the Buddhist Action Plan the Buddha laid out the necessary foundational element for all other things — the presence of suffering. If it's there in the world as a constant, why not use it? In the Buddhist way of approaching problems, whenever we encounter something that makes us angry or defensive, we first recognize that something is occurring. We then sit with our self concerned mind. By looking at the roots of delusion in this way, we can then see that we react negatively when those roots are not fed. For example, when we hear others putting down gay people, we can see that it is our ego that needs us to be recognized. We react negatively because we want to be liked, recognized and supported. Our ego's compulsion for recognition makes us look outside ourselves for the source of our unhappiness. It wants to blame our unhappiness on others.

The *Dhammapada* talks about how the mind will struggle desperately when parted from its usual sources of sense gratification. It will struggle so much to retain *Mara* that it is like a fish taken out of water and thrown onto land. Yet if we lay the blame squarely on the primary cause — our own ego-attachments — our experience of problems becomes Dharma, and our suffering becomes virtue. This perception of suffering as virtue is mentioned in the *Song of Enlightenment*:

> *When I consider the virtue of abusive words, I find the*

scandal-monger is my good teacher. If we do not become
angry at gossip, we have no need for powerful endurance
and compassion.[23]

In other words, we see suffering as supporting the generation of the
path to enlightenment and happiness within our minds. In this way,
we use suffering, it does not use us. Problems become like food. We
take them in and transform them into energy. This involves
consciously training the mind to see the benefit of situations and as
opportunities for practice. This takes time and consistent effort, and
is not an easy practice.

When I first read Case 97 'Getting Despised' in the *Blue Cliff Record*,
a collection of Zen *koans*, I had an instant reaction. Also known as
'The Diamond Cutter Scripture's Scornful Revilement,' this *koan* is
as follows:

> *If a good disciple is despised, it is because*
> *in a previous life there was some transgression.*
> *But if in this life he/she bears it patiently, the*
> *compensating merit will cause the transgression*
> *to be extinguished, and the patient disciple will be adequately*
> *recompensed by the final attainment of enlightenment.*

There are two understandings of this. Firstly, to clearly realize your
true self is to expiate karma. This is because if we truly know the
emptiness beyond absolution, we see that the real *Diamond Sutra*,
the source of the above quote, is our essential nature. This means
that the only indubitable way for our karma to disappear is to
realize that our true nature is totally empty. Negative karma can
only operate in an atmosphere of separateness, of self and other —
of *me* doing this to *you*. Self-centeredness always generates karma.
Knowing or being essential unity however, allows us to embody
non-harm because we act from an awareness of no one to be
harmed and no one to do the harming.

---

[23] From *The Diamond Sangha Daily Zen Sutras*, ©1991 by Robert Aitken. Reprinted by arrangement with the Diamond *Sangha* Zen Buddhist Society, Hawaii, USA.

For this reason, when we realize the true nature of reality and hence, our own nature, we turn the sutra, it does not turn us. In this way we become the *Diamond Sutra* itself. This is what is meant by the final attainment of enlightenment. Secondly, a literal interpretation is that karma can be extinguished in the present age by virtue of the fact that revilement and scorn leads us to employ appropriate and positive measures (such as the Precepts and The Noble Eightfold Path) to overcome our suffering.

My reaction to this *koan* does not mean however, that I encourage suffering, that I search out suffering or that I'm amazingly happy when I suffer. If I did I would question my mental health. What it means is that I am extremely grateful to have experienced problems because without them, I would never have faced myself and my own ego. Now is the present, past and future. Now is all we have, and now is the time to deal with our problems and transform our karma. Without encountering ego-threatening situations and people, I would gladly have lived for the rest of my life in the same old way. That way was painful, intractable and inescapable. I was desperately unhappy. That is not the case today.

Turning my mind towards suffering has also enabled me to gradually develop more and more of an ability to be patient under insult. That's a skill gay people can really use. To be patient, keep our ordinary mind, and be unaffected by the disapproval of others, is extremely hard to do but positively utilitarian in its effect. The importance of patience as a skill is stressed repeatedly in many Buddhist writings. As the *Sutra in Forty Two Sections* makes clear, great power lies in patience under insult. Those who are patient do not feed resentment. This sutra explains that the strength of patience under insult is great, because those who are patient do not harbor hatred. It also points out the benefits of patience. That is, patient people gradually grow more peaceful, strong, calm and resilient.

Many other sutras also praise patience, and outline the fact that reliance on patience is a great refuge. Patience is compared to a soldier's armor, a life saving medicine or the raft which will carry us across troubled waters. The *Dhammapada* states that a true Brahmin is one who endures abuse, violence or punishment without resentment, and whose power and protection is patience.

In Buddhism a Brahmin is a 'worthy one,' a person whose heart-mind is free of mental defilements. Patience is a skilful way of acting and being.

For this reason, patience is considered *kusala* — skilful action. We can see this in the many sutras that deal with ethical behavior. From the traditional Mahayana viewpoint, there are various dimensions of patience. Ordinary patience, for example, involves learning to endure whatever life throws our way. That is, the mundane problems of being in a human body.

Transcendental patience enables us to center our belief in the Triple Gem, and to embody those qualities considered illustrative of a fully realized person. Interestingly, it is this type of patience, the patience which emerges from meditation and mindfulness, which enables us to cope with physical abuse, humiliation, put-downs and any other negative action arising out of the three roots of delusion. There is nothing at all to indicate gay people cannot acquire this patience.

Sometimes however, letting go is not totally possible and neither is patience. It takes practice. For me a good example of this was the first few years of driving to work after finally accepting that I was gay. As I commute, there is always plenty of time for my mind to turn over the issues of the day. In those early years I bailed and bailed out the boat. Since there were one or two people who really bothered me with their homophobia, my mind would replay over and over what they had said. As a counter-measure, again and again I would recognize this and then drop it, only to have it resurface a few seconds later.

Sometimes I would be so exhausted by the time I got to work that I'd fall on the steering wheel completely worn out. Other times I tried Zen Master Thich Nhat Hanh's *Driving Meditation*, in which the stop lights of the car in front of me would be the signal to stop thinking and bring my mind back to the present. This was only half successful. My mind and ego are strong willed.

We are only human and we cannot let go constantly. So what do we do if our intentions are skilful and we've been bailing and bailing for a long time, but still all we want to do is hit someone? The answer: We just float.

Letting Yourself Float

There are times to bail and bail, and there are times to pull up the oars and let it all hang out. The fact is that there will never be an end to bailing out the boat. This is the First Noble Truth of Buddhism — life will never be as perfect as we want it to be. Women have made great strides in equal rights but sexism still remains. So too have African-Americans but racism still exists. Though we may make attempts at creating a permanent reprieve, it is the nature of the world that it cannot be totally achieved.

This kind of practice is especially useful to gay people because it lets us realize that there will never be an end to homophobia, because if this is our goal, it is an unreachable one. It is easy to miss this fact. As the *Dhammapada* reminds us:

> *There never was,*
> *there never will be,*
> *nor is there now,*
> *someone who is always blamed,*
> *or someone who is always praised.*

When we focus too much on constant practice and intentional action, there is the danger of overloading our expectations, and we become people with an acquiring mind. That is, we keep a constant eye on what we get out of practice rather than just practicing. We think that what we will get is a state where we will never be angered or bothered by homophobic people, or that there will come a day when they will all like us. This misses the point. By accepting constant practice as a constant, it no longer seems to be a thing separate to us. There is nothing to cut out of our lives. Everything becomes practice. Accepting the First Noble Truth allows us to stop struggling and losing energy through our opposition to reality. We must realize the truth of suffering if we are to see life as it really is.

This is not to be taken as submission to life's misery or a defeatist axiom because the Third Noble Truth, that there is a solution to suffering, offers hope. If we interpret this solution not as the extinction or severance of suffering but as the removal of separation from suffering, then the reason why becomes apparent. This might be splitting hairs, but is a useful angle for us to take because it doesn't mean rejecting, crushing or snuffing out our suffering — it emphasizes living in and with our suffering.

In this way we do not suffer anymore because there is a crucial difference between getting rid of suffering in the former way, and befriending it in the latter. When we see suffering not as separate to our lives but as part of it, it transforms an object that we want to get rid of into something that is intrinsic to us. We befriend and transform suffering by taking it into us rather than excluding it. This is a holistic, non-contentious and non-oppositional approach to dealing with the cause of suffering, and the state of suffering.

To take our suffering into ourselves and to accept it as part of us is to let ourselves float. To float we have to balance but also trust ourselves and the currents. When we float in the sea, for example, we become alert to just floating and our attention is focused on the whole experience — the sound of the sea in our ears, the angle of our bodies, our breathing. We can become aware of ourselves in a concentrated way which does not involve separation of any kind.

This approach to suffering is especially helpful to gay people because it orients our experience towards both accepting and reducing separation through the affirmation of our Buddha nature, and the acceptance that everything, even that which we dislike, is also the Eternal Self. This gradually enables us to move past the confines of our emotions, and is especially useful to those of us who are extremely limited in our ability to publicly express sexuality.

For whatever reasons, some of us are not public with our sexuality. That some gay people are closeted causes disapproval from certain segments of the gay community. Some of us believe those who are closeted are damaging the cause of equal rights, and that the choice to be closeted is a reflection of low self-esteem and/or cowardice. Again, if we have a panoramic take on this, these things may apply or they may not. Whatever the case, we must avoid over-simplification and finger-pointing. Even if we disagree with people's choices, it still remains that gay brothers and sisters are in a particular situation and as such, need practical and compassionate help.

In my case I have always mentioned homosexuality in the context of safe behavior in the classroom but until recently did not talk about it in any other context. This was not only due to the legal constraints of my work, but a personal choice. I felt that if I opened my mouth I would only fly into a rage, be nasty and unreasonable, or feel ashamed of my actions afterwards. I feared my ego would just fly out of control were I to bring up the topic of gay people. While equal rights requires public action, it was a more skilful decision to keep my mouth shut for a long time and focus more on affirming Universal Mind than on changing others.

This is because the intent to educate others about our experience can backfire. It can be a tricky ego mine field. Gandhi once drew attention to the quality of any intention to change the perception of a dominant group, in his case the British. He stated that the crux of the matter rested upon whether one's intention was to punish the wrongdoer or to correct the situation. For many years I felt both. If I was at all proficient in baseball or wouldn't have been horrified afterwards, I would've gladly taken a swipe at people ripe for the hitting. Those bigots made my blood boil. I felt trapped within a dual framework of aggression and self-righteous hurt, and the wish to achieve some sort of mutual respect. I wanted to hurt people and I wanted to be better than that — I wanted to love them. This confused and angered me, not to mention that it damaged my image of myself as a fair person.

Those of us in the closet know that closeted practice is more difficult. It can appear at times that our only choices are to sit and breathe, and it's natural to think that nothing can come of this. Being closeted is really, really difficult because we are left with ourselves. We can spin our wheels in our own dust very easily. It took me a very long time to keep my head above water on a constant basis. Being closeted is not an easy or preferred environment for practicing Buddhism. At times I have experienced psychological trauma. This is not to say that this doesn't happen when we aren't closeted, but that being in this situation has a high potential for mental harm if one is not careful.

Yet at the same time, like any situation in which suffering occurs, there is the potential to learn important things about ourselves and our situation. In my case, I learnt to face my fears and anger. This does not mean that I am suggesting that being closeted is a good way to practice, or that I am recommending or justifying it. It is simply the observation that we can get something out of any situation if we want to.

What I discovered was that there is a way to make being in the closet beneficial, provided practice is at the forefront of our minds. I found that keeping quiet allowed me the space to develop skilful attitudes and behavior. For example, I made an effort to develop a sense of curiosity about the homophobes at work — who are they? What do they mean by what they say? How do they know what they think they know? What kind of people are they? Every couple of months I'd choose a new person and try to gradually get to know them. Sometimes this made me feel really uncomfortable, and when that occurred I'd back off. I only did what I could handle. But this did allow me to make some interesting discoveries.

There are many things gay people can learn from observation and mindfulness in a closeted environment. By just sitting with what is happening, we find out very quickly how people feel about gay people because they think we are not one. People can be very open if they think they are in a homogenous group where they will not encounter social disapproval. We can also come to see that the people who are homophobes are deeper than their prejudice.

They have all manner of things to talk about, and possess redeemable qualities like any other people. When we suffer we often want our attackers to be one-dimensional because it's easier to attack back, and because we hurt. But Life just isn't that one-dimensional. The truth is that bigots can be wonderful people in many ways. True, they are not wonderful towards us, but it still doesn't mean that every aspect of a homophobe is negative. Neither does it mean that we should accept their prejudice or wear rose-colored glasses. It does mean however, that if we totally write them off for being homophobic, it is no different to them writing us off for being gay. Either way, the total is judged by the partial.

A partial view also distorts the dimensions of homophobia. When we are hurting things can seem more frequent and bigger than they actually are. So, for example, we experience prejudice once a week, but see it as 'happening all the time.' While I am not minimizing how terrible prejudice can be (once is enough in anyone's lifetime), if we take each moment as it comes, the dot in the square remains just that.

The dot in the square is an old pop-psychology test of the 'glass half full/half empty' sort. It's not rigorous in any way but can be a general indication of our mind-state. In a square on a piece of paper is placed a small black dot, and a person is asked what is in the box. Most of us see just the dot, but in fact there is the space all around it. The inference is that we tend to concentrate on negative incidents in our lives and forget all the other moments before and after them. The darker times seem more obvious because we focus on them. We do not see the balance. I now see that there are more non-homophobes on staff than not, more equality in younger generations than not, and more times than not when I experience joy rather than pain.

I also found I could gradually deepen my insight into Buddha nature. This is completely possible in any situation, included closeted ones. In my type of practice, which focuses on affirming Buddha nature, mindfulness equals seeing and letting go. This means that when we are in the midst of suffering, we don't have to do anything. Instead, we can just watch. Anyone can learn, as I did, that we don't have to come up with world shattering theories and plans for change, all we need do is be present.

The old (and oft repeated) Zen axiom is 'eat when hungry, sleep when tired.' So when we are angry, we just be angry. When we are hurt, we hurt. We try not to insert ourselves into the hurt and we don't create add-ons to the situation. Neither do we fuel victim-conceit. If you tend towards the obsessive and overly self judgmental as I do, this can sometimes seem a monumental task. It's difficult to do because it's so simple but we complicate it with thoughts and fears. Yet as the *Dhammapada* observes, when you don't insert you, then there is no you in amongst it all. And when there is no you there, you are nowhere. It just is what it is. Just this in itself, is the end of stress.

So if we cry, the tears fall. We do not reject or encourage. We just cry, and then attend to the next moment. It is all the Eternal Self, even the homophobia and even the violence. Practicing in this way means we can bear witness to our daily suffering and still be whole. We don't have to ignore or suppress anything. It means that what can seem unending and unendurable can be made endurable and workable.

Sometimes it is overwhelming to think that there will always be disapproval or opposition to who we are. Without doubt, the equal rights train is coming to town and change is on the way, but that may be decades away and its arrival date unpredictable. It will not totally remove suffering from our lives anyway. Only a transformative practice and attitude can do that. With the above approach gay people can find a way to integrate all experiences into a constructive framework which incorporates the pain of separation into the acceptance of wholeness. Pain will always be present, but it has been re-framed through panoramic understanding.

As Zen Master Rankei Doryu once pointed out, it is not that you sweep away ordinary feelings and bring into existence some holy understanding. The panoramic understanding of where pain sits in the scheme of things is an eminently practical and ordinary thing. Knowing that everything is Universal Mind puts out the flame of hate and enables us to lay down our burdens. We see that we are not alone because there is no one to be separate and alone. We see that we don't need special Buddhist accoutrements to help us. In fact, there is nowhere to go and nothing special to do. All we need to do is be. What a relief.

Again, I can see my teacher shaking her head at all these concepts because until we really see reality, this is indeed the case. Unless practice makes real a wordless and intuitive understanding of this, the above are just words. Yet it still remains that any gay person can awaken, and any gay Buddhist can receive guidance from their teacher and fellow practitioners in how to realize all of this for themselves.

The end result of this approach is described in the *Dhammapada*. That is, that those who live in the Dharma rest in happiness in this world and the next. We sleep easy because if we drink in the Dharma, we live happily with a serene mind. As the *Visuddhimagga* also reminds us, having sprung out of the unconditioned, the Noble Path is inexhaustible, and it is a deliverance which comes from being free of the attachments which cause worry and stress. As is usual with anything worthwhile however, this is no easy thing. There are no free tickets or rides. But the reality is that Buddhist practice does narrow the gap between what we read in Buddhist books and our everyday lives.

12
Narrowing the Gap

When considering our practice as Buddhists, it is useful to recognize and accept that there can be distance between doctrine and experience, especially in the early stages of our practice. Yet the most important task for Buddhists is to work on narrowing this gap. The message to take from this book is please don't give up. Relief will come. If you fall down seven times, get up eight. There can be times in the lives of gay people when just about everything seems overwhelming and finding the way out seems an impossible task. When the gap between the wonderful words we read in Buddhist Primers and our own negative feelings seems insurmountable, we can remind ourselves that practice *can* make our lives full of joy, and that there *are* a multitude of forms which successful practice can take.

In fact, such is the efficacy of practice that even if we aim at something else we can still hit the target. When I came out and was completely overwhelmed by the experience, I could not think of or put into place any strategy which seemed to work on a long term basis. Just as one wave would engulf me, another would be swelling in anticipation of attack. The system which created and enforced homophobia seemed too intractable and too powerful. Buddhist practice was new, and even though some of the techniques worked, I still could not look bigotry in the eye and breathe it. It was just too much. It was at this time that I decided to work with what I could work with — me. Other things would be tackled later.

My hope was that, by concentrating on me, the rest would take care of itself somehow. That is, by shooting the arrow at myself, the target out there (homophobia, prejudice) would be hit. And it has been in so many ways. When I began practice everything was separate and disconnected. After ten years, I know that the target and the archer are not different. That is why this approach worked, even though there are many other types of practices which work equally as well.

We don't have to know how they work either. For sure, Buddhist sutras and teachers can tell us quite well how they do work. Yet often in our daily lives we conceptualize teachings and the meaning becomes obscured. It's at times like this that we have complicated matters. I know when this has happened to me because a voice in my head says, 'Hang on. I don't get that now.' When words seem untranslatable to daily life, it is useful to know that practice will narrow the gap regardless of whether or not we understand how this actually happens.

The Buddha stated that as meditators we cannot know how much of our ego or how many of our attachments are wearing away daily. We just have the knowledge that they are. He rightly observed that we cannot point to an exact spot and say, 'There is the catalyst,' or measure transformation with a yard stick. But change does occur. It occurs not so much *in* our lives but in how we *relate* to our lives.

Some people say that each of us has one or two *Life Koan*s. A *Life Koan* deals with key questions each of us must answer if we are to live the life of a realized person. Ten years ago my *Life Koan*s were 'How I can be happy under these conditions?' and 'How can I live as a gay person in a straight world?' I believed it was my life task to work on this. This has changed into just 'What?' I cannot concretely explain this and I am still answering it, but somehow it seems right. My original *Life Koan*s have transformed themselves into something much more open and curious.

Without doubt, I'm still angry, and I will always be angry at injustice and inequality. I have no hang-ups about this anger. It comes and it goes. The difference these days is that for the most part, I don't get as hooked so often or for as long. As my teacher says, it's whether you accept it and breathe with it, or hang on to it and perpetuate it. The longer I practice, the more I feel the ease that comes with knowing that this too is Dharma. By 'this' I mean even that which hurts me. Sometimes I fall off the bandwagon and sometimes things still get stuck in my craw. Sometimes I am the best horse[24] but more often than not, the worst horse. I am still ego driven, and full of constructs and concepts, just less so each year. Yet my aim is to always follow my friend's advice and 'get over myself.' This can be achieved by any gay person.

---

[24] Best and worst horse — in the Pali Canon the Buddha compares living beings to four types of horses. The best horse will run of its own volition and without the use of a whip. The second best runs at the sight of the whip. The third runs when it feels the pain of the whip, while the fourth and worst horse responds only when the pain penetrates to the marrow of its bones. The pain of the whip is a metaphor for suffering.

Recommended Books

I have found the following books and articles particularly helpful in my practice.

Theravada and General Introductions to Buddhism

Armstrong, K. (2000). *The buddha.* UK: Weidenfield & Nicolson.
Bancroft, A. (Ed.). (2001). *The pocket buddha reader.* Boston: Shambhala.
Buddhist Missionary Society. (1993). *Gems of buddhist wisdom.* Malaysia: Buddhist Missionary Society.
Hagen, S. (1998). *Buddhism plain and simple.* USA: Broadway.
Jacobson, N. P. (1970). *Buddhism: The religion of analysis.* USA: Southern Illinois University Press.
Khema, A. (1999). *Be an island: The buddhist practice of inner peace.* USA: Wisdom Publications.
Yun, H. (2009). *Being good: Buddhist ethics for everyday life.* Taiwan:Buddha's Light Publishing.

Zen

Bayda, E. (2003). *Being zen: Bringing meditation to life.* USA : Shambhala Publications.
Beck, C. J. (1993). *Nothing special: Living zen.* USA: HarperCollins.
Low, A. (2000). *Zen and the sutras.* USA: Tuttle Publishing.
Magid, B. (2008). *Ending the pursuit of happiness: A zen guide.* USA: Wisdom Publications.

Specific Approaches to Suffering

Berzin, A. (1998). *Developing balanced sensitivity: Practical Buddhist exercises for daily life.* USA: Snow Lion Publications.
Bayda, E. (2000). *At home in muddy water: A guide to finding peace within everyday chaos.* USA: Shambhala Publications.

Chodron, P. (1994). *Start where you are*. USA: Shambhala Publications.

Chodron, P. (2001). *The wisdom of no escape and the path of lovingkindness*. USA: Shambhala Publications.

Chodron, T. (2001). *Working with anger*. USA: Snow Lion Publications.

Dhammananda, K. S. (1996). *Why worry? How to live without fear and worry*. Malaysia: Buddhist Missionary Society.

Hawley, Kipp Ryodo. (2009). *Three steps to mindfulness: Bringing zen awareness into your life*. USA: CreateSpace.

Kabat-Zinn, J. (1990). *Full catastrophe living: using the wisdom of your body and mind to face stress, pain and illness*. USA: Delta.

Kabat-Zinn, J. (2005). *Wherever you go there you are*. USA: Hyperion.

Martin, P. (1999). *The zen path through depression*. USA: HarperCollins.

Perez, I. S., & Wick, G. S. (2006). *The great heart way: How to heal your life and find self-fulfillment*. USA: Wisdom Publications.

Rinpoche, L. Z. (2001). *Transforming problems into happiness*. USA: Wisdom Publications.

Salzberg, S. (1997). *Loving kindness: The revolutionary art of happiness*. USA: Shambhala Publications.

Sunim, D. K. (2005). *Wake up and laugh: Dharma talks by seon master daehaeng*. Republic of Korea: Hanmaum Seonwon.

References

Aitken, R. (1991). *The diamond sangha daily zen sutras.*
http://www.ciolek.com/WWWVLPages/ZenPages/Daily-Zen-
Sutras.html

American Association of Physical Anthropologists (1996). *Statement on the biological aspects of race.*
http://www.virginia.edu/woodson/courses/aas102(spring01)/art
icles/
AAPA_race.pdf

Author unknown. The sutra of forty-two sections (Samuel Beal
trans., 1862). *Journal of the Royal Asiatic Society, XIX.*
London:Harrison and Sons.

Author unknown. *Sayings of the buddha, the iti-vuttaka* (J. H. Moore
trans., 1908). New York: Columbia University Press.

Author unknown. *The dhammapada: A collection of verses; being one of
the canonical books of the Buddhists* (F. M. Muller. trans., 1881).
Oxford: Clarendon Press.

Author unknown. *The sutta-nipata: A collection of discourses: being one
of the canonical books of the Buddhists* (V. Fausböll trans., 1881).
Oxford: Clarendon Press.

Author unknown. *Vinaya texts part I: The pâtimokkha, the mahâvagga,
I-IV* (T. W. Rhys Davids & Hermann Oldenberg trans.,
1881).Oxford: Clarendon Press.

Author unknown. *Dialogues of the buddha (the digha-nikaya)* (T. W.
Rhys Davids trans., 1899). Oxford: Oxford University Press.

Author unknown. *Psalms of the early buddhists: 1. psalms of the sisters*
(C. A. F. Rhys Davids trans., 1909). Oxford: Oxford University
Press.

Author unknown. *The udana, or, the solemn utterances of the buddha, translated from the Pali* (D. M. Strong trans., 1902). London: Luzak & Co.

Bancroft, A. (2000). (Ed.). *The buddha speaks: A book of guidance from the buddhist scriptures.* Boston: Shambhala Publications, Inc.

Goddard, D. (1932). *A buddhist bible: the diamond scripture.* (1st. ed.). Vermont: Dwight Goddard.

Santideva. *The path of light: A translation of the bodhicharyavatara of santideva* (Lionel David Barnett trans., 1909). http://www.sacredtexts.com/bud/tpol/ index.htm

Schloegl, I. (1975). *The zen teachings of rinzai.* London: The Buddhist Society.

United States Department of Energy and the National Institutes of Health. (n.d.). *Human genome project information.* http://www.ornl.gov/sci/techresources/ Human_Genome/ home.shtml

Warren, H. C. (1896). *Buddhism in translation: Passages selected from the buddhist sacred books and translated from the original pâli into english (visuddhimagga).* Harvard: Harvard University Press.

www.ingramcontent.com/pod-product-compliance
Lightning Source LLC
Chambersburg PA
CBHW030023290326
41934CB00005B/466